ON THE STREET

A MELBOURNE ANTHOLOGY

Quiet Corner Publishing
105/40–52 Percy St Brunswick VIC 3056
ABN 21 236 425 289
www.quietcorner.com.au

Published by Quiet Corner Publishing in 2020.

A catalogue record for this work is available from the National Library of Australia

ISBN: 978 0 9954469 2 2

Cover design and illustration by Alyssa Coombs.
Typeset in 12/18 pt Adobe Caslon Pro by Alyssa Coombs.
All photographs taken in various streets around Melbourne.

on the STREET

a MELBOURNE anthology

edited by

SARAH FRASER & SUSANNA NELSON

CONTENTS

INTRODUCTION

Susanna Nelson

Melbourne streets. Surely characters entire within the pages of countless well-received pieces of literary fiction? Surely a subject well represented among the non-fiction shelves of the city's many bookshops? Surely – to be blunt – done to death?

Well, yes and no. If, as iconic Australian architect Robin Boyd mused, our built environment is an allegory for ourselves, then those streets are as ripe for dissection, for yearning, for eulogising, as any plot or character device.

The city is in a state of constant re-imagination; it has always sported, cheek by jowl, an endearing muddle of architectural styles. But Melbourne's built environment has changed beyond all recognition in the last decade, spurred on, for better or ill, by a penchant for new spaces, for minimalism, for subdivision, for higher density, or in pursuit of a knockdown–rebuild opportunity. Blink and you miss things – historic pubs slip away in the hands of greedy developers, for whom the insubstantial fine is a mere tax on the way to greater profit; flimsy apartments go up, while infrastructure crumbles away.

When a piece in this collection prompted a brief recollection of the old Gas and Fuel Corporation buildings – two brown seventies suits that stood, knock-kneed, where Federation Square now commands attention – my response was visceral. I never went inside them. They held no purpose for me. But they were part of a formative mental imprint of Melbourne, the city of my youth. They are now molecules; air. They only continue to exist as long as some of us still remember them.

All the lost buildings, vistas and locations that star in this book are ours, collectively and privately. We have moved through them, cycled along them, danced in them, huddled in their dark recesses until the dawn breaks outside, clutching sustenance, alcohol, friends or lovers; been sick on the bluestone outside. Even if we have merely admired them on our way through, they remain imprinted on our memories. They exist in our imaginary, even if they no longer exist in the physical world. This collection is testament to that existence.

26 February 2020

...

Sarah Fraser

This was supposed to be a very different introduction. It was supposed to be a breezy yet meditative commentary on place, our connection to it, the metaphor of "the street". Perhaps I would have talked a bit of something about memory and how the streets, the city, written about in these pages exist both geographically and on another, psychological, plane. How Melbourne's streets are inhabited by four million people, and each of us has a unique map of them. I might have mentioned community, and how, far from being mere means to get from A to B, streets are where the life of a city happens.

However.

As I write, our streets are disorientatingly silent. A global pandemic means they are forbidden to us. At least, forbidden to us for many of the pastimes written about in this book. No shopping, getting drunk with mates, spewing, avoiding past lovers, meeting new ones, watching crowds, hugging strangers, stopping just to look. People scurry along the streets, heads down, faces covered, mostly alone. They walk with purpose, getting from A to B. Our maps are shrunken, utilitarian.

We don't look up, we don't linger; we certainly don't gather. Without people, the streets have lost their personalities – they are stripped back to their most basic function as thoroughfares.

And so, this book has become, quite accidentally, a celebration of public and private life in a time before COVID-19 and lockdowns and social distancing. It's astounding to see what we took for granted. The essences of place that we thought were simple truths – the rowdiness of Brunswick Street, the hustle of Swanston Street, the street-side coffee and sunniness of every other main street in Melbourne – aren't essential or true. They can disappear, actually, in a matter of weeks.

At the beginning of lockdown, I said to a friend that this book now felt like a wake, rather than a celebration. It's like we wrote a birthday speech and ended up at a funeral. I was being melodramatic – this book is definitely a celebration. As Sue has said, Melbourne is always changing, asking us to adjust to a different reality – this is just another, bigger change to get through. COVID-19 has taken our streets away; we can only wait patiently until they are returned to us. In the meantime, I hope these stories are an optimistic reminder of what awaits us.

19 April 2020

ACKNOWLEDGEMENT OF COUNTRY

We acknowledge the traditional owners of the land on which all these stories are set: the Wurundjeri and the Boon Wurrung people of the Kulin Nation. We acknowledge the Taungurung people, on whose land this book was edited. We pay our respects to their Elders, past and present.

Melbourne

North

West

East

Inner

South

North

BRUNSWICK STREET

SUSANNA NELSON

I was recently sharing anecdotes about Brunswick Street with my guitar teacher. He's a guy in his mid-fifties – his glory days on that street run parallel to the punk and sharpie heyday of the late 1970s. For context, I am someone in slightly earlier middle age. I was hanging around Brunswick Street in the early 90s – I did go on a teenage date to Mario's in 1988, but I had no idea I was "on Brunswick Street" in the way that I did later, so that doesn't really count.

Anyway, my craggy guitar teacher was lamenting the demise of no fewer than "six live venues and six guitar shops" since his youth. We counted them on our fingers. Though I could not verify that there were indeed six guitar shops back in the 1970s – it seems an excessive number, even for Brunswick Street – I was able to count well more than six live music venues I had visited in my time on Brunswick Street and in the immediate area that were no longer there. Interestingly, with a few lauded exceptions, they were entirely different places to those my teacher named. It's fair to say that neither my guitar teacher nor I had regularly frequented Brunswick Street for some fifteen years in my case and, well, probably closer to thirty in his.

My point is that Brunswick Street's utility exists in time as well as place – it exists at different points in our memories. This might be true of any street, but the "live now, pay later" vibe it has always exuded is really only of interest to the young. Youth is Brunswick Street's tribe, and there are few people at either end of that bell curve who have much to do with it – certainly my guitar teacher has moved beyond its main target market, but even I, saddled with young children, no longer have much business there.

The eternal teenager of Melbourne streets, Brunswick Street has always been "too much". While change and reinvention is a constant in the vibrant inner north of the city, the hipster café minimalism of nearby Smith Street seems to have bypassed Brunswick Street, which now has a tired, dusty feel, and a patina of 90s design elements that it can't seem to shake off – all tile mosaics and wrought iron and gold leaf and curly typeface. Brunswick Street seems a shadow of its former self, a relic from my own past, but perhaps to someone more culturally astute it also offers the sense of being one step behind.

Overlapping gaudy shop fronts compete at eye level, while Victorian facades loom above. What is visible of the original brickwork is, in places, ornate and gothic, rising up several storeys towards red and white spires; elsewhere there are reminders of the more modest single-fronted workers' cottages that characterised old Fitzroy before the Housing Commission swept them away, installing instead the imposing tower blocks on the corner of Gertrude Street.

This first reckoning with change inevitably made the remaining terraces, which still line surrounding streets like Napier and George, seem luxurious by comparison to the neighbouring high rises, and eventually they became a much sought-after commodity. Of course, decades of gentrification didn't hurt.

When I was a regular to the area, Johnston Street – or Elgin Street at the student end – was like an artery pumping lifeblood through various iconic thoroughfares of the inner north. As a very new university student, you might first venture as far down Elgin as Lygon Street to sample a prosecco and a big bowl of pasta, or glide through the various taverns that dot that route on your way further down to Nicholson Street. If you were braver and had more time on your hands, you might walk down towards the famous Brunswick Street, along the section of Johnston that is home to the Laundry, Hares and Hyenas, the Portuguese deli and, once upon a time, the Bull Ring and the Spanish Club – places that served small, loyal, diverse communities for many years. These days, cavernous health clubs and a Coles reveal the changing interests – commercial as much as social – of the strip.

Stealing away from campus to the solace of Brunswick Street was a favourite pastime of mine in the 1990s. You could throw down some coins (never a note – it was rare to have one or need one) on a coffee at the Black Cat or a beer at the Punters Club and that was the price of entry for a day spent lazily watching a band rehearse, or conversing with other Converse-attired denizens of the street, or finding a bargain in the op shops that still existed there in exchange for a few more of your coins, or making a mental note of a desirable record in Dixons and vowing to snap it up before someone else did.

Back then there were constant rumblings of impending gentrification. The arrival of chic fashion stores like Rich and Gorman was cause for consternation, as was the street's gradual evolution into an eat street from its beginnings as an all-purpose hanging out, gigging and drinking street, which once boasted the independent radio station, RRR (located on one of Brunswick Street's many tributaries), tiny galleries and the arthouse Panorama cinema.

But it was when the Punters Club – that eternally sticky, dank, dark and viscerally alive pub at the heart of the street – closed its doors for the last time in 2002 that the doors also closed on Brunswick Street as a place of relevance and accessibility for the sorts of people that generally make a difference to culture.

When the Punters Club closed, the ecosystem of people who brought something more than money to the street – students, the unemployed, artists (and many people would identify as all three at once) – went with it. As always with the gentrification process, the less-talented, more cashed-up fans of Brunswick Street's promise of bohemia flooded the area, sending house prices and rents soaring and, in a final irony, lodging the noise complaints that were a stake through the heart of the street's rich live music scene.

Closer to the city, near the housing commission flats, the street's working-class roots still show. Along this stretch there is a soup kitchen and a legal aid centre, a modest supermarket, a tobacconist and a plethora of long-tenanted restaurants frequented by locals who share a historical and cultural affinity with the cuisine on offer – Ethiopian, Nepalese, North Indian, Burmese. But as you move down the hill away from this neighbourhood, this sense of cultural community dissipates. At the point where you reach the intersection with Johnston Street, the ever-louder clarion call to youth - in all its fickle consumerism and contrived eccentricity, and its need to move on to the next shiny bauble - takes full effect.

Perhaps this is what is wrong with Brunswick Street in 2020. On the day I visited – a Wednesday – the street felt as deserted as the CBD of Melbourne often feels on a Sunday. "For Lease", "Retail Opportunity" and "Auction" signs dotted the street. The bars, restaurants, gelati and crepe shops that cater to tourists and weekenders were empty or closed. Capitalism remade Brunswick Street in its own image; being affluent became a precondition of entry, and the life drained gradually out of the street. It now seems to be struggling to capture a new generation.

Walking along the street, past all the ghost signs yet to be replaced, I noticed the old Ministry of Style outlet, for years an institution. It is difficult to think of a more niche "youth" commodity than the ludicrous dayglo rave gear that used to hang on the unisex mannequins in the (now deserted, along with all those guitar shops) window. The same could be said of Polyester, that den of books where well-thumbed volumes on bondage photography and dead punk rockers lined sale tables.

In some ways, the mystery is not why these subcultural haunts have now disappeared, but how they managed to stay afloat for so long. I count myself lucky to have spent time letting my still-growing brain feast upon this long-departed, half-remembered version of Brunswick Street, and I'm sure my guitar teacher does too.

Brunswick Street
by CHRIS MUIR

CTORIA
VB

MIKE'S BUCKS' NIGHT MEMORIAL TOUR: ANNIVERSARY EDITION

Brunswick Street, Fitzroy

SHEILA GRAHAM

Gertrude St Tram Stop – 9 pm

OK, OK, everyone settle down . . . Is everyone here? Come on mate, we haven't got all day . . .

I just wanna give a bit of background about the tour to start with. So this is a historical tour run by me, Trent, and just so ya know, all the proceeds from the tour go to the Melbourne TAFE foundation – That's the "Trent's getting Absolutely Fucked, Eh" foundation! Ah come on, mate, I'm just yankin ya chain, don't be such a fucken stupid girl about it! So, a bit of historical context – eight years ago tonight, me best mate Mike had his last night of freedom before getting . . . I don't wanna say anything negative about her because he's actually asked me to stop making comments like that about her, but the best word for it is *shackled* to Jen. So this is just to show ya the sights of that night, and hopefully to tell a story of a bygone era, ya know, of a past where ya could go all weekend with ya mates and sleep in the disableds on Monday without some stupid bitch phonin your mate every ten minutes saying that you were supposed to be going up the coast to see her fucken . . . dying nana or some shit.

I started this tour as like, an *homage* to a bygone age so we can remember an era when you were able to go out and actually have fun, because you're not really allowed to do anything fun now because you've got kids now and all you've got to say for yourself is "for fuck's sake Trent, ya can't keep calling here at three am on a Thursday, I left all that stuff behind me years ago." And I gotta say, I know that if it were up to him, he'd be right here raging with me, but he's off at some wedding reception in Kangaroo Ground with, well, I don't wanna say "her" but let's just say some bitch who happened to get pregnant JUST before we were all going to Bali for a massive one.

OK, has everyone got a can? And . . . One, two, three . . . SCULL! OK, gentlemen, start your engines!

So as best man, it was my role at the time to make sure he had a fucken great night. So I got the blokes together, and Brandon, and I was all, let's fucken go for it! Chicks, coke, beers!

So. This site here is where we began the tour – Gertrude Street tram stop. We'd had a few cans on the tram the way – Does anyone need another can, by the way? Good – Well, I'd had a few cans on the tram, anyway. Mike and Brandon and James were like, "Nah, Trent, We can just wait til we get to the bar, can ya put that away? Someone might see us". And to be honest I was feeling a bit stressed at this point. I mean, like I said at the time, we used to do this every Saturday, smash a few cans on the tram. And then Mike came out with all this crap about how we were sixteen then and now we're all in our thirties, and I was just like *glug glug glug*, ya know? Just fucken going for it. And James was looking a bit nervous about being in the big smoke so I tried to put him at ease, just like telling him to relax, and telling him to stick with us, and like getting him in a headlock and stuff because he's from Christ knows where out in the sticks and he's not too used to the city, so I just wanted to make it fun for him. Then Brandon's all like, "Calm down mate, he's just a kid, let's go and have some dinner." And I'm like, "I thought this was supposed to be a stag? Who the fuck wants to eat food?" Plus I'd already had a bit of nose powder so I was good to go. But gay blokes like Brandon are a bit sensitive and stuff so I didn't say anything else in case he fucken started crying or some shit. Also Mike was starting to look a bit tense at that point so I was like "fucken fine let's go to the Provincial. But I'm not eating."

The Provincial – 9.20 pm

So we go in and IMMEDIATELY Brandon's all like, "How do you like Melbourne so far James, what's been the best part of your trip, are you planning to study next year", and all that shit, so at that point I had to step in. I mean, nothing against fucken gay blokes like him, ya know, it's fine that they've, ya know, got their own bars and stuff, but James is just a kid and the thing about Brandon is that sometimes all ya have to do is look in his eyes and all of a sudden time just stops and you feel like you're the only two people in the world, and that anything is possible. But that's not really fair, the way those blokes do that to ya against ya will. And James is just a young bloke so it's not fair to him so I had to step in and demand everyone do shots. Which no one did except me because they all wanted to try the specials or some shit, and I'm still like, "Is this a fucken stag or what? I mean, I thought we'd left that bitch at home but she might as well be here for all the fun we're having" and then Mike started raising his voice about how he's asked me three times now tonight and he doesn't expect to have to ask me again. And obviously I had had a few by that time so I was just like "Why are you even marrying her anyway? Remember Janet? What happened to her? She was a fucken laugh, PLUS she thought I was great AND she thought it was great that we still went out and raging AND she fucken left us alone because she realised that we were fucken mates and that's the main thing."

And Mike puts on his "quiet voice" and gives it all, "Janet has twin boys now and she lives in Hong Kong with her husband and works for KPMG. We're not twenty-one any more mate, I dunno why it's so hard for you to accept that this is what I want now". Poor bloke – basically lying to himself just to save face. Glad I'm not like that! I mean, I was with Susan for like, what, five years or something? And she never expected me to NOT go out raging, or come home before midnight, or have sex with her or anything so I dunno why Jen's acting like such a cunt because Mike obviously prefers going out with me.

So they all had dinner and I just sat outside and smoked and had a few beers for two hours. Because if no one else was going to take the stag seriously then it was up to me.

The Evelyn – 11.30 pm

So once they'd finished their fucken . . . spaghetti or whatever, Mike's calmed down and he looks like he's loosened up a bit so they came and got me from the bar, and they were like "OK let's go and get some beers! Time to party!" I think. Because I was pretty smashed by then – had to go and have a tactical chuck in a doorway while they were eating. And when I got back they looked pretty pissed off but I think that's because it was clear by that point that I was having the best stag ever and they had to catch up because they thought it was better to waste time by having a meal or a fucken conversation or something. So we go to the Evelyn, and we're in the queue and I'm having a laugh with some chicks in front of us, asking them what their names are and where they're going and if they're fucken hookers and stuff, and Brandon starts acting all tough and holding me back, and all like,

"That's so offensive, I'm so sorry about my friend." And then get this, he asks me to apologise!

And like I said, I don't have anything against blokes like him. It's fine that they can get married to their, you know like their boyfriends and stuff, but sometimes when he puts his hands on ya, it's just like you feel totally invincible and like it's just you and him against the world and like you could be a king. And I'm definitely not a fucken poof or anything like that so I don't see why I should have to "Moderate my tone" or whatever it fucken is Jen says, ya know? So I apologise to them and they're all uptight after that, even when I was saying "I'M SO SORRY" in a sort of gay voice, so I just have to stand there with Brandon's strong powerful hand on me arm.

So we get in to the bar and there's some band playing, some gay-looking blokes and a woman on drums for some reason. So James gets the beers in and I'm like, FINALLY we can have a good time. So I start getting into it, having a dance for a bit. Then, because as I've said it's a stag, I was like, "Why don't we do a few lines?" So Mike's like, "Mate I would normally but we've got James with us and he's just a kid really so we should go easy for now". So I'm on me own in the disableds racking up after that and I'm just like, what sort of stag is this anyway. If it was just me and Mike we would be fucken going for it at this point, just going and going until we blacked out and then anything could fucken happen, ya know? No questions asked! And no explanations required.

Then just another tactical and out to the bar. But they were watching the band by that point and I just had to just hang out on me own and try and make sure the stag went off.

Coles – Midnight

So I have to go out and get some cash and Brandon's like, "I'll go with you". Which is great, but the thing about blokes like Brandon is that sometimes when it's just you and them they do this thing where it's like an explosion of butterflies in your heart. So we're just standing in the queue and Brandon's all, "I know it's hard for you and you feel like you're losing your best friend. But Jen's a good person and they make each other so happy. Her parents are coming for dinner next Sunday, and we're all going to be there. You should come."

And he puts his hand on me shoulder and I just had this weird feeling like I've not had since I was a kid, like your eyes wanna take a piss but there's someone watching? And he puts his hand on me shoulder again and then my eyes DO start pissing out fucken tears or whatever and Brandon's giving me shoulder a little squeeze and then we just stand there, silently. I fucken dunno mate it was almost like we had some sort of connection or something. So then I fucken saw some chicks crossing the road at the Seven-eleven and I was like, "Hey you cunts German? Cuz I can tell ya both lookin for a sausage!". And then Brandon just shook his head and walked off and I was like "What's your fucken problem?"

Unknown laneway – 5 past midnight

Yeah that's where I had another tactical.

Polly – Time unknown

So after a while the blokes DO get into it. Mike got a round in, James started talking to some chick at the bar and I helped him along by shouting "HE'S A FUCKEN VIRGIN, HE'S A FUCKEN VIRGIN" across the bar, ya know just so she knew he wasn't a player and that, but I felt a bit weird after that whole Brandon thing. Like I said, it's FINE that they can be in parliament and stuff – that Penny Wong seems like a good chick – but I was starting to think like it's weird for a bloke like me to have a feeling like that for Brandon. And I'm pretty fucked up by this point mate, so I just say to him, Brandon I dunno what it is mate but I just feel very drawn to ya. And I don't mean in like a gay way just like man to man. And Brandon, he's just giving me this look, that I dunno mate, I just felt like I wanted to dive into these deep brown eyes of his and like, just have a swim around in his mind? So I says to him, I says, Brandon, I think it's fine that guys like you can adopt kids, with your . . . Partners or whatever, and then from then on it's a bit of a blank, to be honest with ya.

Me work made me get some sort of therapist – total bitch, I think she's a lesbian or some shit to be honest with ya, she doesn't even wear make up – and she's giving it all this "Do you think there's something about your feelings for your male friends that go beyond friendship? Perhaps there's something else there that you could think about until our next session?" So I'm like no fucken way, so I quit! I'm not having some woman tell me to think about fucken feelings or some shit. That's fucken discrimination.

So nowadays this is me fucken job – I mean, yeah it was OK working for the bank – health insurance, so-called therapy, ya know, getting paid – but for now I'm just happy going up and down Brunswick Street, just showing other blokes how to have a fucken great stag.

LIMINAL SPACE

High Street, Westgarth

RCWR

My first and only tattoo is a monkey; golden furred with an electric expression on his blue face. His jaws are open to show a sharp-toothed maw, half laughing, half snarling. He has lively black eyes. He has climbed to the top of my right shoulder and hangs there from one hand with his claws digging into my back. Where his claws dig in, blood trickles from the gashes in my flesh.

It's not meant to be subtle.

I got the tattoo at Black Mark, a studio on High Street, Westgarth, by a stellar artist called Crispy.

The studio – near the corner of Westgarth and High Streets on the second floor, accessed (appointment only) by an unmarked black screen door with an intercom – is gorgeous and almost gratuitously hipster. Every artist has their own space decorated with inspirational paintings, reference material, bad taxidermy, different kinds of tattoo guns and art supplies, everywhere that the eye falls to rest is full of colour and difference.

The monkey tattoo had been in my thoughts for a long time.

...

There are recurring themes when you write about your life. I talk more about my childhood than my teens or early twenties. My childhood was filled with unmappable strangeness, so I write where the discomfort is.

...

I had lived back in Melbourne for over a decade before I returned to Westgarth, keen to transfer the monkey from my mind's eye into reality.

Before that, the last memory I'd had of the area was the drive there in Dad's '87 Corolla: across the bridge over the Merri Creek and then up the gradual incline of High Street's commission flats and old office spaces and warehouses. The arterial road travels north into Westgarth, warded on either side by rockery walls, crowned with twin canon and an honour guard of elms.

This grand entrance to Westgarth was envisioned and built in the 1880s as an attempt to instil espirit de corps in the locals, but when I was a kid, as soon as you got to the beige pebble toilet block (a syringe-ridden cesspit that only the desperate attempted) at the intersection of Westgarth and High, the illusion was roughly dispelled.

Westgarth is tiny. It's not a suburb in any legitimate sense to do with boundary lines or post codes or the rare addressed envelope, but it's got some pretty cool history.

The Wurundjeri people of the Kulin Nations count the area as part of their traditional territory. Pre-gold rush, Merri Creek was a lush spot, and the land around it was important to the Wurundjeri for food like freshwater mussels, as well as shelter, travel, and the use of certain trees for tools and ceremonies.

Around three blocks to the south of the tattoo shop, John Batman and then Elders of the Wurundjeri are believed to have met to discuss a "land use" agreement – the only such one ever attempted after the European occupation of Australia. Without a hint of irony, the agreement was disavowed by the English because if they ratified only one land agreement, there might be a perception that occupation of

Australia-entire was unlawful. Thus, inexorably the land was changed, the mussels and the useful scarred trees annihilated, and almost all evidence of this past was lost except for records and stories still told by the Wurundjeri.

...

The monkey had been in my mind since I realised that I could get a tattoo. There was no doubt that it would be a monkey, that it would be on my back, that it would be angry about something.

Initially it was to be small little monkey – the size of a walnut. I thought that its very tininess would be a symbolic understatement, a comment on the wild emotions I sometimes find myself struggling with, but which I always smother, not a hair out of place to be seen by anyone except those who know me well. But as I grew more comfortable in my mind, more aware to the facts of myself, the monkey stopped being a cheeky mouse-sized kid's cartoon; it enlivened itself and grew wilder.

For my thirtieth birthday, my partner, Kris, having listened to me longingly describe monkey an untold amount of times, made the grand offer of paying for him as a gift. The shock of a dream becoming reality is still with me. The cost had always been beyond my means, and I had consigned monkey to grow only in my imagination.

I wasn't ready for the rush of emotion when I realised my ideal artist was in High Street, at the point where life had become so uncontrollably volatile and strange.

...

I was five years old when my parents and I moved into Westgarth. The house was three blocks to the north from the current site of Black Mark tattoo studios. It was the first and only non-sharehouse we'd lived in, and we were all a little uneasy at the prospect.

Like most houses in the area, built for poor immigrant families after the gold rush, it was a small, uninsulated weatherboard cottage with concrete steps and a four-square-metre front garden. The house had three rooms and felt empty and silent in comparison with the riot of noise and energy at our previous place in Carlton with its five people and revolving door of guests.

But I soon fell in love with the wide quiet back streets, the seemingly endless stretch of grass next to Merri Station, and the fact that you could see the sun setting. A sight I'd never known in the inner city.

In my memories, Westgarth in the early 90s is an endless drought-stricken summer, punctuated by a lot of serious talk about El Nino. It wasn't the artfully arranged be-treed delight that it is today. The tarmac roads, sticky and smelling of ozone, absorbed every degree of heat and burned my bare hippy feet as I ran from shade spot to shade spot. In the summer, the heat and dry, caustic winds served only to make High Street more interesting, filled with laconic people in various states of undress.

Westgarth is one of those areas whose only purpose seems to be the establishment of a liminal space: it's really part of Northcote, but the community don't see themselves as Northcotians. Northcote lives at the top of the hill. In the downhill, one always refers to Westgarth.

The establishment of these tiny non-suburbs, it's said, was an attempt by inner-city dwellers to keep and enhance a sense of small-town community that was lost as Melbourne expanded during the gold rush. The attempt worked, and the area is one of the few areas, like Kooyong, that has repelled the rapacious entity of greater Melbourne.

In the 90s, Westgarth (and Northcote), of which High Street, with its regular trams and buses, was like a lifegiving river, felt like an eccentric haven away from both the banality of working-class culture and the stilted, elitist fixations of the rich. It was a relatively well-meshed society made up of elderly Europeans, young Chinese families, Anglo inner-city hippies and artists and a thriving queer community.

My iconoclastic, theosophical, beatnik parents gravitated towards

Westgarth like salmon swimming upstream. They couldn't really afford it and they'd exhaust themselves trying to make it work, but it was the only place for them to be at that point in their lives.

...

As a child, the understanding of mental illness in others comes in the form of rituals.

You learn the nuances of expression and body language; the soothing activities particular to each person in your life; the very real dangers of a prejudiced and ill-educated society, and, most importantly, how to de-escalate. The pointlessness of anger and recriminations. In short, the methods to the madness.

My parents, as a result of their quite separate, different symptoms, were very vulnerable people. It made them susceptible to the Pandora's box of human maladies.

Mental illness creates great unbreachable chasms of confusion in families. When someone you know closer than blood and skin and breath, someone who thinks and talks the same as you, becomes strange – not a stranger, yet – it's like watching someone you know from across a vast distance.

In some ways you can become closer, because vulnerability entices protectiveness and co-dependency, and you can find that paranoia and hysteria are contagious spirits. In other ways, that great distance has the hollow feeling of betrayal.

...

I needed two steps for each of my partner's long strides walking up High Street as we waited for my tattoo appointment. I had wanted to show Kris a street filled with the bohemian charm of my childhood, but I was disappointed. The shabby chic that I remembered – which is still somewhat maintained further north – had been swapped for the bland trappings of established wealth. In many ways it was more distressing to see the institutions that were still there – but irrevocably altered to conform to the new population.

The organic shop, once a small, bustling and brightly coloured grocery that stocked sourdough, silken tofu and the occasional carob "treat" had transformed into an immense warehouse and taken over at least two shops, now distributing floor-to-ceiling multivitamins, protein bars, essential oil moisturisers and vegetarian prawn crackers.

Similarly, the Valhalla Cinema, a name which had sparked a lifelong love affair with Norse mythology before I was ten, was now part of the Palace chain and had been renamed The Westgarth. I didn't go inside.

The City of Darebin's greenie flair was still around, but even the robustness of the well-watered gum trees and thick Australian grasses that had grown up in traffic islands since I was last there felt smug and crass. The old spiky tea trees that had once grown in gardens and on corners everywhere in the north, looking dry and unkempt, were gone. Replaced by more sightly silver gums with pink flowering gumnuts.

...

It was at around the age of seven that I started realising my mother and father were different to other parents. They didn't seem to have regular friends. People would come and go quite quickly in their lives, often unexpectedly, and the friends who persisted were infrequent and often lived outside of Melbourne.

It became clear when the rituals I had been taught, the ideas and modes of dealing with the world, didn't check out in reality. Also, the cracks were starting to show. Sudden rage spirals and deep unshakeable gloom made unexpected appearances; my dad started making a loud beeping noise when he felt overwhelmed, or confided to people "I'm going to die"; my mother had wild manic periods full of grand predictions. They soon separated, unable to deal with their own selves, much less the concentrated support needed by the other.

Despite the separation, we didn't leave Westgarth, which was now a lifeline for me in its stability. The ongoing strangeness and the depth of understanding that I needed to offer my parents had made making friends very hard. In truth, I had only one friend, and her afterschool schedule was so strict we rarely saw each other.

I lived with my mother in a sharehouse three blocks to the east of where Black Mark tattoo studio is today. We'd shop almost exclusively at the organic shop. It was the first time we'd ever tasted sourdough bread and we devoured the flour-coated loaves in thick, buttered slices whenever we had a windfall. Our favourite accompaniment was pumpkin soup, "spaced out", as my mother called it, with potato to save money.

High Street became a sort of character in my life. I could shop at the organic shop and safely discuss food and cooking with my mother – something that dominates our discussions to this day – and I could on occasion coax my father out of the house for a five-minute walk to the op-shop. It was a Safe Space, as things are termed today.

The trams and trains would rattle by on all sides of the tiny non-suburb, their regularity as comforting as the purring of a cat.

...

I wasn't unhappy. The deep-seated distrust of an inconsistent world that I developed during the four years living in Westgarth was tempered by the fierceness of the love I was surrounded by. When one parent was too bizarre to handle, the other would most likely be there to comfort and distract. I was their only child, beloved and needed. Indeed, quite often the mania and delusion made them full of unwarranted and grandiose praise.

When we left finally Westgarth, off into a whirlwind of fraught experiences, the lifeline that was the tiny little non-suburb was lost to me.

Coming back to the same place to get the monkey tattoo, I wandered with my partner for half an hour up and down old streets, unable to recognise my old home.

. . .

As a teenager I had wanted my monkey to be angry; sick to its stomach with confusion and energy spent and opportunities lost. When I went up the stairs to Black Mark studio, drawing in hand, I just wanted him to be wild, taking up space, alive.

MY HOME PAGE

Separation Street, Northcote

RIJN COLLINS

I sat in the car, scowling. My boyfriend tried to coax me out, but he knew how defiant I could be. It wasn't just that I considered the drive so far from the city, it was that I considered it . . . well, so ugly.

My spirits were already low at the prospect of moving to Northcote, but they sank even further when we turned into Separation Street. Litter caught in the chain link fence of the rubbish tip fluttered as we drove by, in a grim wave of welcome. We slowed down near a small graveyard whose cracked headstones were only a few metres from the footpath. I swung my head towards Paul in a slow-motion stare of pure reproach. I was twenty years old and acting like it.

One month earlier, when he'd suggested living closer to his studies at La Trobe University, it was the first time I'd even heard of Northcote. He took us on an exploratory drive; I cried the whole way home to Richmond. Where were the punk squats and record stores, the live music venues and bookshops? All I saw on our ride north was bleak suburbia. I wanted no part of it.

It did make logistical sense, however, not to mention financial. In the early 90's the bleak suburbia of Northcote had considerably lower rental prices than urban, gritty Richmond. And so we stopped the car outside an "Open for Inspection" sign and unclipped our seat belts.

"Separation Street," I muttered when I finally opened the car door. "Hope that's not an omen for us."

It was. We did indeed separate on Separation Street, our tenancy outlasting our relationship. But what flourished was my eventual love for not just my rubbish-dump-and-tombstone street, but the whole area.

Northcote in the early 90s was not the hipster haven it is now. Far from it. The only element of funk it displayed was deposited way down the southern end in Westgarth, with its arthouse cinema and handful of cafes. In the twenty-three years I lived in Northcote that funky aspect began a slow creep up High Street, bringing with it a new wave of vintage clothing stores and cocktail bars. It changed the whole dynamic of High Street, like a chain of fairy lights flickering on, one by one. Bar Nancy, the Wesley Anne, the Social Club … this new lease of life altered the atmosphere of the area (and the rent prices), but did not quite reach Separation Street.

Despite my initial grievances, it didn't take me long to feel utterly at home looking out at the gravestones from my bedroom window. The appearance of the street was deceptive; extremely narrow, it nonetheless connected the Eastern Freeway to the northern suburbs, and so brought a constant thrum of traffic past us. It didn't help that there was no nature strip. Walking home from Bi-Lo loaded with groceries meant keeping my elbows tucked away from car doors whizzing past. That walk would also take me past the rubbish dump, once a brickworks. By the time I moved on it was being transformed into the enormous All Nations Park, which would change the face of the suburb.

Across Separation Street from the rubbish tip was the Northcote Library. It was here that I formed some of my fondest Separation Street memories. When Paul first showed me this new thing called The Internet, my contrary nature once again rose to the surface. So you could search for any information you wanted, and find it straight away? I could barely use my hairdryer, and so hid my intimidation behind a sneer. "Sounds boring," I remember saying. "It won't last."

Fast forward several months, and I would often be standing in the queue for the three computers the library offered, waiting for my half-hour Internet booking. I would print out each and every email I received, whisking them away from the prying eyes of librarians to tuck inside my bag and take home to read. I was a member of two feminist punk collectives, helping publish zines and organise workshops. There were at times several hundred members, so the pace of the printing would often be frenetic. The noise of the dial-up modem is pure nostalgia, alongside the frustration of having the line drop out, again and again. But lord, the bliss of curling up on the couch with a glass of cask wine, and a thick wad of emails to read through!

The neighbours were not without interest either. On one side we had Joe, who blared Elvis tunes all through summer nights and claimed he'd once sung with the King himself in Vegas. On the other side was a halfway house that had frequent police visits, and whose alarm would shock us awake in the middle of the night. Once I pulled my curtain aside to come face to face with a youth stuck half-in, half-out of a window opposite, limbs flailing.

We both froze. I nodded politely; it was all I could do not to utter a brisk "Good day, sir." He nodded back. Even as I closed the curtain I could hear the sirens.

I became so enamoured with Separation Street that when we were eventually given our marching orders from the landlord, I just moved seventeen houses down. Our first home there had faux wooden wall panelling that we covered with Sid and Nancy posters and layers of cat hair. The kitchen floorboards were so rotten than a misstep would twist limbs and invoke curses. The rot got so bad we had to outline the sagging patches with masking tape to identify them, and do an odd hopping dance of avoidance every time we wanted to turn the kettle on. I think we lived that way for nine months. In the Great Tradition of Landlords Everywhere, when they did finally listen to our requests and came to inspect the floor, they realised the enormity of the repair and kicked us out to do it.

I found us another rental house down the road. It was so close that I just filled garbage bags with my clothes, tied them to the handles of my bicycle, and rode them down the alleyway to my new back door. This second house soon held a solid wall of punk posters, and barrels of fermenting home brew whose distinctive "bloop" noises were strangely comforting as I drifted off to sleep each night.

We had a spare bedroom that became our study when I followed Paul's lead and enrolled at La Trobe University. He was right: Northcote was an ideal location to get to campus. The number 250 bus took me past the beautifully kitsch Northcote Bowl near the north-eastern corner of Separation Street, a blue brick Modernist building with an enormous rooftop bowling pin tipped on its side. Local residents came out in full force ten years later when it closed down to watch in a reverential hush as Betty Marlborough, the face of the control counter for twenty-five years, bowled the official Last Ball. The building squatted between the corner 7-11 that fed our late-night snack needs, and the YMCA whose façade still brings the tang of chlorine to my nostrils.

My bag swollen with linguistic textbooks, I would alight from the bus after lectures and duck into the 7-11 for a packet of Alpine menthol cigarettes to "help me focus". I shared my essay writing time between our spare room and Northcote Library, through whose large glass doors I watched Northcote Plaza gradually grow in size and scope. The view of Separation Street from my house was less grand; stray litter from the rubbish dump flitting along the footpath and the clog of impatient drivers. Early one morning I watched from my study as a neighbour ran into traffic in her terry towelling dressing gown and held up a frantic hand, palm out.

A car skidded to a stop inches from her legs. Was there an emergency – what could have happened? I leaned forward, ready to react. She ran to the driver's side and feverishly mimed smoking. It took me a moment to register. Was she really running into peak hour traffic just to plead for a cigarette? She was indeed. The driver honked in outrage and she jumped out of the way. I moved my own packet of Alpines out of view, just in case.

When I needed a break from studying I would walk to the cemetery. Many of the graves were German, bearing names such as Kupsch, Müller and Fritsch. I had formed a fondness for the grave of Private AE (Alf) Barker, who died in 1915, aged eighteen. Under his name were two poignant words, *peacefully sleeping*, missing the worn *a*. I often curled up cross-legged next to Alf and shared my thoughts with him. I placed flowers on his grave, and poured out a tender glass of whiskey on the grass next to his resting place on the anniversary of his death in a loving libation. I told him quietly of the changes in the world, and in me.

It was in our Separation Street lounge room that my housemates and I sat transfixed while the TV brought the pivotal events of the 90s to our couch. We set our alarms for 3 am to watch the live feed from LA as the OJ Simpson verdict was announced, and sat in silence watching the funeral procession of Princess Diana wend its mournful way across a grieving London. It was the death of Kurt Cobain that hit me hardest, though, little punk at heart that I was. I curled into a ball in my ripped stockings and army boots, and sobbed myself hoarse that this gentle, quiet man had found the world so unbearable that he fought to leave it.

The inclination was not unknown to me. When I first moved to Separation Street at the age of twenty, I was juggling a cocktail of medications designed to keep that inclination at bay. By the time I left it at twenty-eight, my spine was straighter, my armour a tighter fit. Separation Street had seen me step over the line from sullen youth to assured adult, single for the first time in ten years and about to learn sweet, sweet lessons about freedom and solitude.

It wasn't an easy exit. Both the man I was leaving, and the street, had lodged in my heart. The former I knew I had to let go of, but the latter held on tight. Paul and I had reached the stage where the arguments went on for days, and the resentment even longer. We once left a friend's house in St Kilda in the middle of one such heated exchange. Not wanting to argue in front of the taxi driver, we decided to keep walking until we'd calmed down. We walked the whole way home to Separation Street, all twelve-and-a-half kilometres of it. We argued the entire way.

And so I unpinned my feminist punk posters and divided the books into his and hers. I'd been so against moving to Northcote, yet now couldn't bear to be away from it. My new house was off Westgarth Street on the southernmost edge of the suburb, a safe distance away from Paul at his own northernmost edge on Separation Street.

Apart from nine months living in Brussels, I would end up spending the next twenty-three years with my home on the same beloved page of the Melway, the iconic Melbourne book of maps with Northcote on page thirty. Neither of my Separation Street houses have been knocked down in the interim, neither of them renovated. They're pretty much as I left them, in an area that has changed in almost every other conceivable way. Sometimes I walk down my old street when I visit the area; sometimes I don't. But the next time I do, I've decided, I'll take a little detour, curl up next to Alf, and tell him more stories.

SYDNEY ROAD: AN INVENTORY

Sydney Road, Brunswick/Coburg/Sydney

SARAH FRASER

Towards the end of the submission period for this anthology, it became clear that something was up. As we received one piece after the other, a perplexing absence was apparent. We'd had pieces that covered the CBD, suburban streets and quite a few in between. Lygon Street, Brunswick Street and other inner-northern icons were all adequately represented. But . . . where were the odes to my beloved Sydney Road?

Where were the tributes to one of our city's greatest tributaries, a street that could quite legitimately claim to be 878 kilometres long?

Sydney Road, my heart! What did people have against you? Is it your 40 kph speed limit? Your crushed, crushingly slow peak-hour trams? Or is it only that you span so great a range, geographically, culturally and economically, that you defy attempts at description within a 3000-word limit?

Baffled, I realised I was going to have to do it myself. It appears it's up to me to introduce you to the best street in Melbourne.*

Firstly, the name, somewhat controversial for a book about Melbourne.

*Yes it is.

Sydney Road is, indeed, the road to Sydney (which city, you'll possibly not be surprised to hear, doesn't have a "Melbourne" road). Unlike many street names, it is both practical and promising. I, for one, like streets that are named for geography. This road tells me where I might end up, if I were to follow it to its natural conclusion. Let's start, however, at its beginning.

The morphing of Royal Parade into Sydney Road always struck me as one of the most incongruous intersections in Melbourne, where genteel, leafy Parkville, free of such coarse necessities as shops and industry, ran smack bang into the working-class mélange of Brunswick's factories, discount fabric shops and sticky-carpet pubs. The only other place I can picture a similar class abrasion is the join of East Melbourne to Richmond where Wellington Parade meets Bridge Road. (Why is it that wealthy suburbs have parades while the rest make do with roads or streets? Why is it not Dandenong Parade, Springvale Parade, Bell Parade?)

Even now, no-longer-working-class Brunswick presents a shabby face to Parkville. Possibly shabbier than it used to be, with the former Sarah Sands hotel currently boarded up, awaiting a shiny boutique apartment makeover. This makes me sad, so I won't dwell. Let's move on. We'll leave the Sarah Sands (most recently an Irish theme pub) to her fate. Forget the sticky carpets, the two-dollar Wednesday pints of watery cider, the lax bouncers who benignly accepted fudged ID cards from seventeen-year-old country students. The developers have her now, and we can only hope that what develops isn't awful.

Hop on the number 19 tram with me, and let's do Sydney Road properly. We'll go on a Sunday morning, pre-brunch time, when it's possible for the tram to move at speed (up to 40 kph, anyway). Grab a seat, if possible, or one of those cushioned bum-rests beneath the window. Sway with me as we trundle up to the first stop: Barkly Square shopping centre. Here, help a nonna and her shopping trolley up the steps, and watch out for the student carrying home two bedside lamps and a laundry basket from K-mart. Marvel that the MacDonald's and the massive pokies club are still operating in this hipster heartland.

At Glenlyon/Dawson Street is the Council building, a.k.a. the citadel of the People's Republic of Moreland, in which place, presumably, laws are passed to optimise developments such as that impending on Sarah Sands, only to be bypassed by the developers and VCAT.

Give thanks for the library, and resolve to make it to yoga at Brunswick Baths next Saturday morning.

Shuffle to the front of the tram now, so that when we get to Victoria Street (stop 23) you can lean out to wave to George the cobbler. George has been working in his shop for fifty years, fixing things that people no longer want to have fixed. Even if they did, most shoes are so badly made these days, they can't be fixed anyway. George is thinking perhaps it is time to retire. Remind yourself to get your mum's 1970s cowboy boots re-soled before he does.

As we make our way up Brunswick Hill, gaze with troubled soul at the hulking apartment blocks standing in the graves of warehouses and factories. Despair for Brunswick's character and then wonder at your own complicity in all this. It is the eternal quantum conundrum for tourists and gentrifiers: like the cruise ships menacing Venice, have you ruined the very thing you came for? Is it possible to move in to a place, to claim its streets, to observe its charms, without changing it? Sydney Road is no Venice – but the broad principle applies. Then again, it's folly to expect places to stay the same. Even Venice.

Never mind. Keep moving! As we pass Stewart Street, reminisce about the time you helped a housemate move into the squat at Number 1, next to the IGA, which has gone downhill, but has a decent aisle of pasta. At the top of the hill, open the window to let in the sound of

Afro jazz from Bar Oussou, and the smell of fresh haloumi pies from the fabulously womanned counters of A1 Bakery. Scoff at the bridal shops, if you feel the need.

We begin the approach to Coburg. Sydney Road starts to return to itself, and we breach Moreland Road flanked by spice shops, green grocers, Italian coffee shops and the inner North's last remaining Centrelink (discreetly cross your fingers and look the other way). For a while the shops thin out. Wider-spaced blocks contain warehouses, furniture shops, mechanics. The streetscape, I must apologise, is at its most charmless here. The lack of coffee shops or bruncheries might make you feel uneasy, but fight the agoraphobia and hold out a little longer until we meet a riot of kebab shops, pastry shops and delis and sweep up to the Bell Street intersection. At the sight of Bell's triple lanes and 60 kph speed limit, you might be tempted here to leap onto a bus and head east to explore another of Melbourne's major arteries. I warn you though, buses can't be trusted. You'll be turning down a nondescript dogleg before you can say crappy Pentridge development.

Better to stay on the tram, steadfast and true.

It's not far now anyway until stop 40 and the end of the line. We mostly have the tram to ourselves, having shed, in turn, the hipsters, the young professionals, the students. The young family home-owners are west of us, journeying in parallel on the Upfield train, headed for Merlynston and Fawkner stations and the just-affordable quarter-acre blocks around them.

When we get to the North Coburg terminus, step down onto the road and look north.

The number 19 finishes here, but Sydney Road is just getting started. Not far on, it splits into two, then three, lanes and bears cars through the outer suburbs – Fawkner, Campbellfield, Craigieburn. It carries on through the no-man's land of the latest housing developments and flat plains that only a local could love. It partners with the Hume, riving the heart of Victoria to allow trucks and families heading out for a camping weekend to get out of the state by the quickest route possible. (You could I suppose reach the border more quickly by going due north up the B75, but where would you end up? Deniliquin, that's where.)

It bypasses the town that you were born in, but you can still see the crooked hills and granite that hold it, over to the east. Here, in country often thirsty, and yet also prone to flooding, the pull of the city subsides.

Turn off the freeway and take a detour along a road that writhes around, up and over a scraggly range. In the small valley town on the other side, feel your heart slow and sink into the hills and the trees. The road is dirt. The houses belong eternally to their original occupants, never mind how many people have lived there since. Rest. Remember friends and family who are no longer there, and then turn around and return to Sydney Road, head back to Coburg, or Brunswick, where the car-horn, tram-dinging cacophony rings through your head and heart, leaving no room for nostalgia, for melancholy, or regret.

Grab a haloumi pie and savour it, and thank Sydney Road for what it is here and now, and where it might take you, any time you please.

East

VICTORIA STREET

BEA JONES

To this street of character(s)
comes noodle soup and chopsticks,
thin china and green tea,
new rubber sandals next to bok choy,
the smells of the wok
and sweet and sour pork;
vermilion legs dangling
in a surreal pigscape.
An eclectic mix
of Bacon's grotesque imagery
and Rembrandt's glazed pigment.

Here's pork cake, turnip cake,
beancurd roll.
Bird's nest, taro cake,
ginseng jelly
all duckling yellow.

Gold and scarlet,
scarlet and gold good luck scrolls
hang in spice-filled shadow.
Fish, horses, dragons and frogs
swim, prance and jump
in a jade stone menagerie
where smooth-bellied Buddhas
belly dance in one's palm.

In an Aladdin's cave fringed with paper lanterns,
delicately decadent,
I buy for the I Ching's oracle
three Chinese coins,
wondering what fortunes
have been cast to the wind
through the nothingness of their centres.

SIGNPOSTS

Camberwell, Carlton, Brunswick, Footscray, St Kilda

MARK PHILLIPS

Camberwell

When I was fifteen, my parents bought a house in a quiet cul-de-sac in an affluent, leafy part of Melbourne's eastern suburbs. Up until then, we had lived a nomadic existence in Australia and New Zealand, moving city every eighteen months or so to follow my father on his next posting with the big corporation he worked for.

But arriving back in Melbourne after a couple of years in Auckland, it felt as if my parents were putting down their roots once and for all. My middle sister and I were both in high school now, and our moving days were over.

Ours was a big double-storey cream house, third down from the corner. At the end of the street were private tennis courts belonging to the local Catholic parish, hidden by a high hedge and gate, which was locked to the street's residents, and every Saturday, the kerbs would be clogged with the BMWs, Mercedes, and Volvos of the tennis club members. Sundays were quieter, apart from the constant humming of lawn mowers.

A retired bank manager lived across the road. Once a week, he would trim his immaculate front lawn in dress pants, a button-up white shirt and a tie, his grey hair slicked back with brylcreem, as if on his lunch break from work. The only other kids our age lived next door to him. They went to two of Melbourne's most exclusive single-sex private schools, while we went to the local high school; not because our family was poor, but a deliberate decision by our parents, who had both been educated at state schools.

Underneath the name of the street on the sign on the corner were the words "No Through Road". It might as well have said "Dead End". Suffocated by the WASP-ishness, the stiff-necked good manners, and most of all the rigid conservatism, I felt I didn't belong there, and I didn't want to be there. Around my nineteenth year, the neighbourhood was briefly terrorised by a mysterious arsonist who would set fire to garden hedges late at night. Who would be next? people speculated. Vigilante groups prowled the quiet streets, looking for any strangers loitering in the area. Secretly, I cheered for the phantom hedgeburner. Then he was arrested, and everything got back to normal.

Cheap thrills could be found at the Golden Bowl in Camberwell Junction, a tenpin bowling alley with a couple of banks of video games where the local delinquents would hang out, smoking cigarettes and picking fights. It felt dangerous and exotic.

The Golden Bowl was around the corner from Burke Road, the main shopping strip. Like the wall that divided Berlin, here was the impenetrable border between the alcohol-free area of Camberwell and neighbouring municipalities, and the looser morals of Hawthorn and the inner city. Not a single pub or licensed restaurant was allowed to operate on the eastern side of that boundary. But the city side had no such restrictions, and at the top of Burke Road, across from the railway station, was the Palace Hotel, a mundane pub in a grand Victorian building, but a beacon of life for anyone looking for excitement in this suburban Cold War.

Carlton

I set my sights on a degree from Melbourne University. Not because I was convinced that Melbourne was any better than Monash or Latrobe, but because its ivy-covered bluestone buildings fitted my ideal of a proper university.

It was an hour-long commute from the family home, usually on the number 70 tram along Riversdale Road and Swan Street to Flinders Street and then the number 1 up Swanston Street. This long ride gave me plenty of time to read and listen to music on my Sony Walkman. On the tram, I consumed books from the second-floor library in the Union Building, classics like Kafka, Dostoyevsky, and Hemingway; music biographies; and the new journalism of Tom Wolfe, Hunter Thompson and Joan Didion. This was as important a part of my education as what I learnt in lecture theatres and tutorials.

Mostly, my friends and I spent our free time on campus, but sometimes we would sneak away for a few hours to one of the many pubs dotted around the university: Naughtons on Royal Parade, the Prince Alfred on Grattan Street, or the Clyde on Elgin Street. We'd return to our next lecture in a happy, sodden daze. Less often, we would go to Lygon Street, feeling sophisticated as we twirled our pasta and sipped cappuccinos.

In the late-80s, the common lament was that Lygon Street had lost its spark and the epicentre of bohemian Melbourne had moved a few blocks east to Brunswick Street in Fitzroy. People blamed the arrival of big chains like Country Road and Sportsgirl for killing the buzz, but I found the cocktail of Lygon Street's Italian and Jewish heritage mixed with the academic crowd to be intoxicating and alluring. It was still possible back then to walk past Jimmy Watson's at 5pm and narrowly avoid a minor literary celebrity drunkenly lurching from the front bar back to the university after a long, long lunch.

Apart from books, my other great education at this time came from a radio station broadcasting from a Fitzroy back street. Three Triple R, the epitome of cool, was up several flights of stairs in the Universal Theatre building in Victoria Street. As I navigated my late-teens, Triple R was my most reliable companion, and eventually I felt compelled to hear my own voice on air.

One evening a week, I and a group of other hopefuls would spend a couple of hours in the Triple R studios learning about panel operation, tape splicing, interview techniques and other arcane skills since made redundant by digital technology. Our ambition was the prize of a graveyard shift – 2am to 6am.

We were sent by our tutors to record mini-documentaries, vox popping in Brunswick Street about subjects such as *armpit hair: pro or con?* Afterwards, I would catch the tram to the city and make the long journey home.

The tram stop was on the corner of Johnston Street, outside a shop selling falafels, a culinary delicacy unseen in the eastern suburbs. Waiting for the tram, munching on my takeaway kebab, I would gaze across the road at the Provincial Hotel, my eyes drawn upwards to the window of the ladies' powder room, and I would longingly fantasise about the Fitzroy girls in their vintage summer dresses, scuffed Blundstone boots, their nose rings and forests of armpit hair.

Footscray

For my twenty-first birthday, my parents gave me a three-month Eurail pass. With the money I had saved from weekend, night and holiday jobs since I was fifteen, it was enough to fulfill my great dream of backpacking across Europe and the US.

Overseas, I saw and did things that would have been unimaginable in my Melbourne life. But I was the first of my circle of friends to do the backpacking trail, and within weeks of arriving back home I realised everything was exactly as I'd left it. Moving back into the family home was a humbling experience. The street sign still said "No Through Road", the air on Sundays was still filled with the buzz of lawn mowers. After Paris, Rome and New York, even the busiest of Melbourne's city streets felt empty and wide. And the faces walking towards me were all so white.

The only thing that seemed to have changed was that the girl across the road, who I'd had a crush on since I was sixteen, had a new boyfriend. He was a few years older than her and drove a black BMW, and he was rapidly making a name for himself as a news-breaking sports reporter on TV. Years later he would become president of Collingwood Football Club.

Worst of all, I still had one more year of uni to do, and while Lygon and Brunswick streets had felt exotic and stimulating before I'd gone overseas, now they seemed like second-rate copies of the real thing.

As soon as I graduated, I was on the move again. This time to country Victoria, as a cadet journalist for a newspaper in a town on the Murray River. But my real ambition was to work for a metropolitan daily, and after three years in the bush, my next step was back to Melbourne as reporter for a group of weekly papers in the western suburbs.

Our office was in Barkly Street in Footscray. Leaving the city via Dynon Road, your arrival in Footscray was heralded by the giant Franco Cozzo store at the corner of Hopkins and Moore streets, with the latest in baroque faux gilt furniture imported all the way from Italy. But as you progressively travelled west towards our office and Hopkins Street morphed into Barkly Street, the signage changed to Vietnamese words, the air thick with the aroma of aniseed and chicken stock from countless *pho* restaurants, bags of rice and boxes of vegetables spilling from the doorways of Asian grocery stores. A sprinkling of African restaurants and cafes heralded the next wave of migration to the western suburbs.

Among this transplanted Saigon, like rotting teeth in an otherwise healthy mouth, were the old pubs of Footscray, where at lunchtimes topless barmaids served alcoholic Anglo-Irish male customers, many of them residents of the rooming houses that studded the back streets nearby.

By the time you got to our office, the Vietnamese influence was replaced by the markings of postwar Italian and Greek migration. Down the road was a cake and pastries shop where we ordered our extra-strong espressos each morning from a grumpy Italian princess who was always arguing with unseen middle-aged men doing the baking out of sight but within earshot of the customers. But smack dealers and their customers had also moved in to the area, and we often found used syringes in the car park behind our office.

From the editor's upstairs window we could see into Hoy Heng restaurant, where a box of takeaway noodles and Coke would set you back five dollars. Glancing out the window one day, I saw a black BMW parked outside the restaurant, which I recognised as belonging to the boyfriend of the girl across the road from my parents' house. Inside, he was having lunch with Ted Whitten and Doug Hawkins and somehow, as they finished their meal, I managed to snaffle a quick interview with the two Bulldogs legends on the eve of Hawkins' record-breaking 322nd match.

That Saturday afternoon, a kilometre further west up Barkly Street, Hawkins was triumphantly carried off the ground on the shoulders of his team mates after inspiring the Bulldogs to victory, and embraced at the players' race by the man whose record he had broken.

A year later, we would mourn EJ's premature death from prostate cancer at the same location, and another couple of years later, the Bulldogs played their last ever home game at the renamed Whitten Oval in a torrential downpour, before relocating to the new Docklands Stadium.

St Kilda

I met my first serious girlfriend – who later became my wife – at that newspaper office in Footscray. By that stage I was living above a clothing shop in Errol Street in North Melbourne with a dope-addled musician. He sequestered the front room for band practice twice week, and the living room was mostly off-limits because of the toxic cloud of stale fumes from his home-made bong. My room was at the back, overlooking the little roof top balcony where he grew his cannabis crop.

North Melbourne was a tiny pocket on the edge of the CBD that people went around on the way to somewhere else, and consequently, Errol Street was so quiet, especially on weekends, that it felt like the main street of a country town. In the mid-90s, the suburb was still mostly ungentrified, and the pubs were notorious hangouts for hard-drinking wharfies and recently released guests of Her Majesty. Gourmet delights extended no further than a pie shop and two Chinese takeaways.

I lasted there for about eighteen months before the constant mishaps – the kettle catching on fire, the bath flooding the flat when my housemate passed out with the water running – drove me to somewhere safer.

My girlfriend was living on the other side of town, in St Kilda. She had a one-room flat in an Art Deco building two blocks from Fitzroy Street. Before her, I really only knew the suburb by reputation but I began spending as much time as possible hanging around Fitzroy and Acland streets.

Transvestites and pale street girls in tiny miniskirts worked the corners on Grey Street and its tributaries, and dirty Fitzroy Street had a palpable sense of menace at any hour of the day or night. Junkies and dealers conducted business in shadowy doorways, and the chemist across the road from The George doubled as a methadone clinic. Magnificent mansions had been carved up into boarding houses for single men and women, who ate lunch each day at the Sacred Heart Mission.

Everyone wore black. The hit TV show The Secret Life of Us depicted St Kilda as sunny and carefree, but to those in the know it was more like Berlin's Kreuzberg transplanted to Port Philip Bay: grim, edgy and defiantly alternative.

St Kilda was the heartbeat of Melbourne's live music scene and I was willing to concede that it had also displaced the inner north as the centre of Melbourne bohemia. On a Friday and Saturday night, we could generally be found knocking back beers and shooting pool at the Espy, or watching a band from the sticky carpet of the Prince of Wales. Around midday on Sunday, we'd stroll down to Acland Street for lunch at Café Scheherazade or one of the other Jewish delis; if it was a nice day, we'd stretch out under the palm trees outside Luna Park or stroll along the Upper Esplanade, past the craft market, to the pier and the Catani Gardens.

As St Kilda locals, we had nothing but scorn for the weekend visitors from suburbia and the British and Scandinavian backpackers who invaded our locale. "Tourists", we smugly derided them as from perches in our favourite café in Fitzroy Street. But even then, the tourists were taking over, converting the decrepit old mansions and terrace houses into luxurious homes. The POW had a makeover, and the Espy closed down, then the Greyhound was bulldozed for apartments. Within a decade, most of the old St Kilda in all its deviant, wasted glory, was gone.

Brunswick

I once calculated that by the age of fifteen, I'd lived in two countries, five cities, and eight houses, and gone to seven different schools. It had not been much different in my adulthood. In the dozen or so years since university, I had shuffled between four cities and towns and at least ten different flats or houses. I began to understand why my parents had hit the brakes twenty years earlier.

The year 2004 found me living in the national capital as a member of the Parliamentary Press Gallery. I enjoyed the work in the maelstrom of national politics, but compared to Melbourne, Canberra was really not much more than a large country town.

My girlfriend and I had been saving for a house deposit for a few years. We'd rented a small terrace in Chetwynd Street in North Melbourne for a couple of years after she'd had enough of St Kilda, so North Melbourne was where we began our house hunting.

But after a few months it became obvious that anything but the smallest, most claustrophobic flat, or the most run-down terrace in North Melbourne was beyond our budget. We began to look further afield, and focused our attention on Brunswick, a dozen or so tram stops up Royal Parade.

After two years of looking and a couple of near misses where we'd been outbid at auctions, my partner stumbled upon a renovated single-fronted weatherboard terrace in our price range in a narrow street within walking distance of both Sydney Road and Lygon streets.

I knew Brunswick mainly for its discount shops and Turkish restaurants, but little else. I knew it had a proud working-class history, had been transformed by postwar migration, and now was undergoing a hipster-led renaissance. The same week we moved in, a new café opened in an old milk bar around the corner, named after a Bonnie "Prince" Billy song and staffed by young waitresses and baristas who all looked like they played in bands, made experimental short films or were preparing for their first gallery show.

Our little street is now mostly occupied by young families like ours, although there are still an elderly Greek and an elderly Italian couple among us. The brick warehouses which over the years have served as band rehearsal spaces, housed a taekwondo school, a theatre props maker, and a florist, are about to be demolished to make way for dozens of town houses and apartments. Starting price $900,000.

Our two boys have never known any home other than the one they were born in. Unlike their father, they have had stability and certainty from day one.

I often wonder when they'll feel the same restlessness their father did, a longing to seek out and explore a world bigger and more challenging than the street they grew up in. Their own signposts. No doubt it will happen, and when it does, their father will encourage it because there is nothing more important than forging your own independent path in life.

But wherever they go in the world, they will always know that home is here, in Melbourne.

CROSSING THE TRACKS

Sefton Place, Camberwell

ANNA SUBLET

Tracks

I grew up in a suburb full of boys, in a house next to a railway line. There were the boys who were my friends, and then there were the rough boys.

It always seemed that there were places to go. Our house sat on the corner, overlooking East Camberwell station, where Sefton Place came down the slope past the carpark, sneaking off from the sweeping streetscape of Broadway. From the gabled bathroom window, I could watch the trains pull in and take off again. People flowed from platform to viaduct, above ground and below. Express trains rushed through. The fluorescent lights hummed.

By midnight the line was quiet, with only one diesel freight train hurtling through our walls at 3 am, making the windows shake with the sound of places far away, beyond the suburb, where those covered freight wagons were going.

Just past the viaduct's underground tunnels was the hulk of the old power station. "High voltage" signs marked warnings from the enormous grey walls. Suspended metal walkways, technical signs, the throb of electricity, a promise of links to a grid going out all over town.

We always knew it was there; the buzz and the hum.

The outside zone

Most times I would see the rough boys coming. I watched through the leadlight-rimmed window frames. The glass was warped, making things look wet even when there was no rain. My mother didn't let these boys come inside our house, so we sat on the side steps, the red bricks cold and hard under our thighs as we talked into the night. I had a slow-burning crush on the worst of these boys. His saliva smelled stale when I put my face near him, but I wished that he would kiss me. I can still smell that human tang.

During the days, our neighbourhood gang of friends and brothers roamed the streets on bicycles, dodging commuters and the slow green buses that ran across the suburbs to Deepdene and Kew. We rode in the darkness close to midnight, when it felt empty and quiet, streetlights glowing on the edges of the kerbs. In the pockets of our jeans, we carried our club membership cards, with different coloured ribbons for our respective feats of daring: to race our bikes around the block in under 60 seconds; to ride, no hands, down the Big Dipper; to take off and get airborne from the wooden ramp below the hill. I had earned my ribbon by riding down the Big Dipper, no hands. Those sorts of things. And then, there were other things.

Sometimes we scrambled down to the trainline, paced with heavy, wooden sleepers, the blue-grey jumble of hard-edged granite rock between. We placed twenty-cent coins on the tracks, to see how the trains would crush them. When we returned, the coins had scars torn down their middles. I would finger the ridge and place the coin in my pocket, for safe-keeping.

Coins crushed on metal, the steely smell of blood. I felt I could taste it in my mouth. We messed with such small acts of destruction.

The cutting

The house sat at an intersection point: the railway line diverged, heading off down a dead end to Alamein, or following the main track to Box Hill and Lilydale. Here too, near our corner, the railway met the markings of tracks long gone, bridges and tunnels, old signals and gullies.

The Outer Circle line had left its mark on the landscape, even though the tracks were no longer there. A grand engineering and political indulgence that serviced the line from East Camberwell to Deepdene to East Kew, and from Fairfield to Oakleigh. Passengers travelled this unprofitable route from 1891 to 1927, and then the landscape reclaimed itself, bit by bit. The mapped made unmapped – ghostlines.

The Cutting ran through the gully of this old train line. We charted our paths between the overgrowth of dark trees, and the undergrowth of tunnels and cubbies. Roads ran above us and the brick bridges offered cool, solid relief, damp shelters from the world. Threats and adventure were laid bare there, amongst the tangled branches and the sloping earth. We were skirting a cross-over zone, an opening into an alternative space, train whistles blowing across time. We sought out abandoned houses and clubrooms along the line, the places where things used to be. We burrowed into safe places. We did not stray too far from these lines, the real and the ghostly.

So many ways to hide in our world, when we were just kids.

Mixtapes

Sometimes, the afternoon was spent bouncing on Phil's trampoline. In summer, we did bombs into Martin's pool, swimming laps and racing to the kitchen for cool cordial and biscuits. We made mixtapes and recorded our own radio shows, played songs on keyboards, and hit tennis balls without care.

In the backyard bungalow, we snuck looks at each others' pubes. At night, tents went up in the garden and tapes played until one in the morning. One afternoon by the pool, Anthony kissed me as I lay on my towel. I was surprised by the hot, wet thing in my mouth.

Time travel

Our journeys deviated, after a time. Some of the rough boys started thieving: small break-and-enters. They returned with the spoils of someone else's home. Sometimes they decided to kill or torment small animals. I would see them pull legs off crickets, decapitate a cicada or chop a worm into pieces, with cold intent. One hot day, Ross threw a dart into the temple of my brother. The dart stayed embedded, trembling in his head, as a slow-hanging drop of red blood appeared. Everything slowed, as the sun burned down on the bodies of the tortured insects. There was a buzz in the air.

Our hiding place in the trees became a repository for the boys' porn magazines, buried under twigs in plastic bags. Wet leaves, damp soil. I saw a picture of a naked man carrying his enormous penis on a silver tray, his cock artfully surrounded by roses. Looks of shocked delight adorned the faces of the bare-breasted women awaiting service. Or waiting to service. What did I know of this?

One day we heard about what had happened in The Cutting. A schoolboy had been found naked and crying, "molested". His new watch had been stolen. I could not stop thinking about his tears, with his naked bottom, torn, bleeding; his lost watch and what had been done to his childhood. Time stopped, a little, for all of us.

This train will run express . . .

One day, I suddenly found myself on the other side of the tracks.

"Anna, someone has broken into the house and they have ejaculated all over your pillow." This was the first and only time that I have heard

Mum say the word "ejaculate". "And they have drawn a smiley face in the semen." Time slowed.

I went up to my room, in this altered space, in an altered state. On the pillow was a red pube, curled into the stickiness. A smiley face leered back at me.

Some of my favourite clothes had also been stolen: my Sandi Surf Co jeans, the ones so tight that I had to lie on the bed to pull them on with a coat hanger, and my striped rugby jumper. It was a gang of boys who had done this, I knew. Not just one boy.

All change

When the police came, they took my sheets and pillow away with them, "for analysis". We never heard of any result. I didn't want the bed linen back. For a while, I couldn't sleep in my room, so I set up a wonky li-lo bed on the floor in my parents' changing room, downstairs. The first night brought dreams of boys wearing my clothes, smiling and laughing in my face.

The next morning I looked from the bathroom window towards the train station settled at the elbow of Sefton Place. The platforms had their usual traffic, trains coming and going, people rushing along and below. But there, staring back at me from the station door, was a new piece of roughly painted graffiti: a big smiley face, marking my place.

No longer did I feel I could call these streets and places mine. The crime had stamped a warning on my world. This smiley face was no sign of happiness, but a leering marker. The walk to the Big Dipper went past the viaduct – Who would leer out at me from the dark underpass? Was there anyone waiting in the clump of trees? The plastic bags of porn magazines seemed to buzz from the undergrowth, and the power station throb was a low threat.

It was a whole new world out there. The buzz and the hum. The cross-currents and threats, the promise and the pain. The taste of blood, metal, clothes peeled away, sheets sticky with semen, dark tunnels and all the passings-by of the people. The to and the fro, the horns in the night, those long locomotives dragging carriages packed with goods.

I fingered the ridge of the coin in my pocket, and now it felt like an eruption.

All change, all change.

AIR CONDITIONING
GET A GREAT START!

Inner

A CONSTANT PARADE

AILSA WILD

My first week in Melbourne, I crashed with my pen pal. I must have called him long-distance from my parents' kitchen, but memories skip: from checking for letters at our dirt-track front gate to waking up in his little terrace bedroom. Futon, cheap sheets, laughing because I could see my breath, white, over my pillow.

"Arghhh! Your bedroom's colder than the fridge!"

The rising glee that we lived in the same city, tracing the dotted tram routes on the Melways, share house ads in the Readings window. My hands pocketed in my op shop duffle coat, peroxide blonde kitchen-scissored-pixie-cut, I rode the number 19 to the first place I ever paid rent.

Sitting at the Morrah Street tram stop. Cold. He was achingly late and it was the nineties so all I could do was wait. Furiously bored, I took it out on the traffic, pressing the pedestrian button even though there was no one to cross. Watching the stopped cars with bitter satisfaction. I don't remember if he arrived or not. Or maybe it was a she. Who was I waiting for? But every time I pass those lights, I think of silently, vindictively stopping the traffic.

I borrowed a bike with no brakes, so I had to pitter-patter-run along the ground to slow myself as I headed down past the hospitals towards the killer roundabout. Once I hit a woman. Knocked her clean to the pavement. I laughed at my ridiculous brake-less bike while she lay on the ground.

My friend pulled her to her feet and asked if she was ok with so much concern.

And I laughed.

I still remember it when I cycle past those lights and feel sick.

I can feel free and high on adrenaline, the wind in my face, full of laughter – while hurting another human.

That first spring: the daisies in the grass on Royal Parade. Sitting in the pale sun, finally knowing summer would come, making daisy-chains on the nature strip just up from the cigarette-smell of Naughtons.

Missing beaches and mountains; missing knowing where every shop in town was. But thumbnailing holes in daisy-stems, threading carefully, thinking of my Nana, shrank the homesickness a little.

Balcony. Dawn. We'd been up all night.

We were already laughing before the street-sweeper went rogue. It swung into sight and began doing doughnuts beneath us, swerving round corners so it seemed it would tip over. We clutched each other with delight, like we'd discovered a rare mammal on a mountainside.

Whoever you were, street-sweeper driver, I still love you with all the wild sleepy wonder of that sunrise.

My housemate fell in the bathroom at four in the morning and cracked her head and neither of us had a car, so our friend sped over and drove us to emergency. We jumped out onto the Royal Parade footpath in our pyjamas.

The French doctor's shoes squeaked on the hospital floor and we could hear him approaching like a horror movie soundtrack: "I am 'ere to stitch up your 'ead," and we laughed until I was hurting too. By the time we left, the sun was strangely bright and it was rush hour.

We huddled in the tram, giggling in flannelette and uggboots among the suits.

For years Royal Parade was the way home from the market. I loved the camaraderie of noticing someone's bags on the tram overflowing with silverbeet, celery leaves, kale. The bicycle panniers flashing past, sprouting green. The bulging nana-trolley pulled up at the traffic lights. The weight of paper-wrapped cheeses at the bottom of my backpack. The sense of plenty and domestic achievement in a life where sleep was optional, the dishes pile teetered and nobody cared about pink mould around the bathroom taps. I loved travelling home from the market, laden.

One night I dinked two boys home from the Fringe at the North Melbourne Town Hall. One on the handlebars, one on the rack. Both of them bigger than me. The weight and laughter of them as I pedalled and steered us all home. My spokes cracked. I needed a new wheel but it was worth it for how tough I felt. Being tough was how I flirted.

Neither of those boys were you. You came later.

Or you were so new then it didn't count.

Years of Brunswick and Northcote before we moved out together. Our baby-boomer neighbours gave us their old king-size mattress and we strapped it to the Subaru; no roof racks, so it flopped over the windscreen. I pressed the buzzer to lift the roller door for the first time and you drove us into the car park. Always before, we'd shared rambling weatherboard places with several friends and ragged gardens of tomato, zucchini, basil. Bags of lemons from George and Voula over the back fence.

Now this. An apartment. A balcony. Royal Parade. Just the two of us and a glimpse of the city out the window.

The silence of it.

For the first time in my life I thought: I could manage having a baby.

Here, in this place.

"We're just up the road from the Women's. He can push me there in a wheelbarrow if the labour goes badly."

Not that we had a wheelbarrow – our south-facing pot plants and writhing little worm farm barely required a trowel.

Eight months pregnant, heading to work and the bike was still more comfortable than the rush-hour number 19. Cycling slowly alongside parked cars, bumping my belly with my knees, thinking of the headlines if something happened: "Reckless Pregnant Cyclist Injured . . ."

My friend telling me to be careful: "You're precious, you know."

But wasn't I precious before I carried this child inside?

Walking in the winter dark, preparing my body. Streetlights and headlights and flashing red bike-tails and my mind on my posture: hips shoulders, how the weight of my belly changed the curve in my spine. Cold tip to my nose. The anticipation of it. The waiting.

Camped out in the king-sized bed while my grazed labia, torn perineum and stretched pelvic floor slowly healed. The smell of breastmilk thick in the sheets. Royal Parade trams rattling out the window, the chatter of guests cuddling the baby in the lounge room. Dozing in and out like a hangover, in love like a crush; all-consuming aching, exhausted love.

Waking again to feed the baby and listen to the number 19.

And again.

And again.

The first try with the pram – across the road into Princes Park. Icy cold June day raining on his face and he screamed himself red. In minutes, we clutched him into our arms and scuttled back over the road and up, up, up to our heated loungeroom, to watch the cold trees toss outside the window.

5.27. Sitting on the concrete steps by our letterboxes waiting for you to come home. The daisies again. Thinking: Winter must be nearly over. It just must be. Bumper-to-bumper and the trams spewing passengers at our stop. Baby in my lap, charming the pedestrians. Me. Exhausted and desperate to not be touched; for no human to be within a metre of my airspace. Please, please come home and hold the baby so I can breathe. 5.28.

Walking through the deep pools of shade up to the nearest Sydney Road café. Arms swinging, summer air in my hair, but tethered to home by my ever-filling-breasts, by the small mouth, the tiny stomach, my own anxious care, the needing cry of body for body. But I did have this: an hour of typing like a demon; of making and thinking; of salted caramel French toast with mascarpone and popping candy filling my ravenous soul.

Crossing Royal Parade with the picnic rug and the baby to lie in Princes Park, the luscious low afternoon light. You, home from work with burritos, rolling towards us on your bike, smiling. The crowds began to trickle and then swell until the park was thick with flocking humans and we asked ourselves, "What is *happening*?" Later I realised it was history and we were there; the women's football filled the stadium and people were scaling the gates to get in. The roars resounded in our bedroom until well after the baby was asleep.

The love I have for crowds.

People holding candles to their chests arriving from all directions to commemorate Eurydice. The silent, sombre, loving, bright solidarity of dusk-walking-thousands. Baby at my aching chest. Tears in my throat. Women all around me.

"Look! look!" I am tugged to a halt again.

I wait. Green balance-bike, pink fairy wings, ladybird gumboots, the matchbox police car that needs a nappy change on the grass beside that fascinating beer can which has been there for days. Vigilance because death by car is only metres away. The desperate, hope-crushing exhaustion of this constant proximity of death. My back aching from lifting so his little, reaching hand can press the button at the pedestrian lights. Again. And Again.

Not to cross the road. Nobody is crossing the road.

I smile at the drivers, silently vindictive, and make them wait as I must wait.

It is impossible to travel more than a meter without stopping. Each fence, flower, gumnut, crack in the concrete, puddle, dog, driveway, coffee cup, leaf, street-sweeper, is more interesting than the distant playground which is supposedly for children.

Living on this road gives me a new appreciation for how humans work together. My friend the nurse has begun to tell me stories from the wards and now I notice them, the nurses, in their scrubs, sneakers and lanyards, up and down Royal Parade at any hour, working in shifts to keep us all alive, the expertise of their care systematically unrecognised.

Often I catch the zookeepers walking home in pairs, in their khaki and boots, and it brings to mind elephant poo, hot chips, the beeping buggies that my child loves more than any animal.

The fluorescent orange coats of the tow truck drivers perched in the service lane, four in a row, at 3.47. Sharing a thermos, ready to swoop down on Sydney Road the second the 4 pm clearway starts, to punish the selfish and unwary alike. It's cruel and funny, and unexpectedly heroic – helping thousands to get home faster.

But most of all, I love the women pushing prams with sleeping babies, or babies they're hoping will sleep, or screaming babies who just won't sleep, or pushing empty prams one-handed, holding a baby in the other arm. Biceps of steel. My abdomen turns sweet for every one of them. I want to make tea and fold their laundry and say, "Just lie down for an hour. I've got you."

Today, the apartment is blessedly empty. Someone else is caring for my child.

Tea.

Words.

The heater.

The slow, golden turn of autumn out my window, bringing us towards another winter on that leafless avenue. The avenue of in-between moments that holds layers of my self; my waiting, furious, anticipating, loving, exhausted, gleeful, remembering, silent self.

LYGON STREET

BEA JONES

Where caffeine culture vultures cruise
an al fresco boulevard
past the strawberry, poppyseed, blueberry mousse
trio of terraced facades,
spruikers in waistcoats
lure the epicure to
Il Primo, Piccolo Monde, Via Veneto –
names that caress the tongue like gelato and cappuccino.

Soap bubbles then lagging leaves
float by the lazy tracery of balustrades
and winter trees,
filigreed against stone and sky.

Pediments and parapets
like wedding cakes of stucco
vaunt a baroque opulence.
Below shadowed porticos
fashion flaunts its haute couture.

While the literati and glitterati
promenade leather and gold
an old man shivers, legs bare.
In the cold, a dog wears
a designer-label coat.

To Lygon Street
come Melbourne's famous and infamous,
the pauper and the stars.
Whether by chocolate or crack they die,
they come to granite and grass,
monolith and menorah
in the cemetery city's classless mortality.

A WORLD WITHIN WILSON STREET

Wilson Street, Carlton

SJ LAWRY

In those heady days of the new relationship of twenty-somethings, when he would leave sprigs of lavender and a note on my pillow, we moved into the former share house in Wilson Street, Princes Hill – a tiny enclave of North Carlton. It was an old red brick Victorian house, with a large, cheerful daisy bush in the front yard, its white flowers highlighting the white in the tiled ceramic walkway, and of the curving timber eaves. When we moved out, nearly ten years later, it was as a married couple with two young sons, and all the detritus that came with that circumstance.

The southern end of Wilson Street (its high point) is framed by an entrance to the Melbourne Cemetery, one of Melbourne's oldest, bounded by Lygon Street, Alexandra Parade and Cemetery Road. Only four houses down, we enjoyed the cemetery's quietude. And could cut through it and avoid the traffic, if travelling by bike or on foot into Carlton proper. In the early days I would wander the cemetery, marvelling at the ornate gravestones in the Catholic area, with their etched names and photographs, where plastic flowers never wilted. Many, many graves had disintegrated over time, the stones cracking and sliding, the grass growing over them, protective yet cavalier. Saddest of all was the grove of remembrance for the lost little children, lying alongside a meandering path, under a large eucalypt, where I would sit and think about those bereft families.

It's a quiet place, Princes Hill, and popular amongst driving instructors and their cautious students. Cautious as were we, gently feeling our way into a new life, and each other. Traffic is limited there – unless there is a big event on at Ikon Park (Carlton Football Club's home) – and the streets are wide, with plenty of space for practising parallel parking, and many stop and give-way signs. Many of the streets, like Wilson, are so wide their median strips are features in themselves, host to thick grass, groves of mature trees and, on hot summer evenings, picnickers spilling out from narrow share houses, drinking cheap wine with dips and crackers. This neighbourhood is built for sharing.

We enjoyed getting to know our surroundings. On foot, along the bluestone alleyways, venturing to Rathdowne Street across the rumbling tram tracks on Lygon, detouring to the flaky sweet French pastries of Filou's, or a hangover breakfast of eggs and milky strong coffee at Black Ruby. Sometimes stopping for a lazy Sunday risotto and wine lunch at the Kent, and browsing books at shop that isn't there anymore, after the owner was paid out handsomely and sought warmer bookselling climes.

Most of all we loved our own tree-lined street, our backyard with its crimson fuchsia tree and a front door with stained glass that shut out the world and kept us safe within. The quiet street suited us. We could venture out into the world, catch a tram straight into the beating heart of the city – to work fighting for justice, or to drink beer at grungy bars. But our wooden-floored home at number 7 would always be patiently waiting for us. We didn't have much, by way of things. Boxes of books, my hoarded second-hand clothes and memorabilia (aerogrammes and photographs, mainly). It was a grown-up place for both of us. In a blue-chip suburb with million-dollar homes, neatly maintained gardens and a whiff of the academic.

At the northern end of Wilson Street, at the bottom of the hill, sat Princes Hill Primary School. It meant nothing to us, in the beginning. Just a landmark. We passed it as we travelled along Pigdon Street. Years later my father would be knocked off his bike at that roundabout, by a white car with a driver who hadn't been looking. He was grazed and dazed, somewhat, but otherwise unharmed. It frightened me, though, when it happened. A stinging reminder of how easily things can shift.

Over time, as we settled in, got dial-up internet and a slightly larger computer, we started to talk about the future, about a family. He would ask, as we lay in bed lazily on a Saturday morning, the cold air pressing in under the old rattling windowpanes, if I could imagine it, a tiny baby lying snuggled up, in our old double bed, between us. He would pat the spot on the sheets where that baby would lie. For the first time in my life, I could, just barely, imagine it.

Some months later, some seventeen years ago now, two blue lines appeared on a white strip, a little sooner than we'd planned. And just like that, as though we'd been living in a kind of Matrix reality, we started to see young couples with prams, or slung with babies, wandering the leafy wide streets of North Carlton, smiling at rather than avoiding the young toddlers careening around small inner north cafes. We realised that at the other end of Wilson Street sat a red brick primary school. And inside the primary school was a kindergarten, fenced to keep the generations apart, and a maternal and child health nurse.

The nurse's name was Kerry, she was no-nonsense, and infinitely kind. She walked into our home, within that first week of our having our firstborn home, and marvelled at how peaceful it was, our space, the yellow-painted walls and wooden floors, the "Most peaceful classical music ever" CD I was playing. The space belied my anxiety. About everything. About our baby getting enough milk, about taking him out of the house, in a pram, crossing four lanes of traffic. About me doing it right, this mothering thing. When he wouldn't sleep, and I would walk the wooden hallway for what felt like hours, with him over my shoulder, patting him as he snuggled in, and wake tired, from dreams of losing him in a supermarket, or of him being in our bed when he was not. A blurry, kaleidoscopic time. Fragments of exquisite joy alongside piercing sadness.

We walked a lot with him, our firstborn. And he grew, and he smiled a lot, and we really got to know our neighbours for the first time, the rhythms of life outside the nine-to-five. The school bell, the church bell, the ting of the local milk bar's front door as you entered, calling the owners out from the back room, where Chinese dramas played on TV. The first word our eldest said was *bird* ... "Bir", pointing at a crow sitting on the rusted cemetery fence. Our second-born came home with us to Wilson Street four years later. We were more confident this time, but I felt an unassuageable guilt at our eldest no longer being the sole recipient of our parental affections. But he took it all in his stride. Navigated kinder, and the long walk down Wilson Street to school, on five-year-old legs.

I collected images of Wilson Street on my digital camera, of the magnificent white gum tree that took up a whole front yard on a corner block, the wagon wheel embedded in a fence, a 1970s flippancy, the life-sized dummy on the second floor balcony, and the roses blooming in the stately cottage garden. I dreamed of creating an artwork, an homage to our street, featuring those images and miniature houses, people, trees. I dabbled in some painting classes. But never seemed to find the time to do more than imagine it.

Two years later, the pressure of parenting, finances and having no family support in the state was taking its toll. On our nerves, our moods. Our children were inexhaustible in their curiosity and joy – their passion for clambering up the steps of our neighbours, even as we just walked by, stopping to watch the snails leave their silky trails along the footpath, and then jumping, running, skipping, was relentless. It was time to move; to find a bit more space.

When I told Kerry the health nurse we were moving, she looked panicked. "You aren't moving to the suburbs for a bigger backyard, are you? The parks here are wonderful for kids, as is meeting other families. Kids just need trees, grass, dirt . . . there's plenty of it around here . . ." I could sense her watching me closely, aware of my skate across the thin ice of depression and tendency to isolate myself. I'd already put in hundreds of hours with the boys at the Princes Park playground, a short walk from our home. Especially on those grey, wintry days when the walls closed in, the winds whistled through bare deciduous trees and the kids were fractious, and all I wanted to do was sleep.

I reassured her that we were only moving up the road, to Park Street. The Moreland side, not the Yarra side. But close enough, still. To the primary school, and eventually the secondary school. As I scrubbed the yellow and blue walls of our old house with sugar soap and wiped the glass back doors free of tiny fingerprints one last time, I felt deep sadness. My life has been full of unhappy moves, after loss. But this time there were also tendrils of hope pushing up, like tendrils of the purple-flowering *hardenbergia violacea* (Happy Wanderer), an exuberant native climber I'd planted out back. A promise of new beginnings, on a new street, in another old red brick house with high ceilings. This time it was wisteria growing, and the floors were carpeted. The boys somersaulted all the way up the hallway, marvelling at its length.

COASTING

Canning Street, Carlton

SARAH FRASER

To stand at the top of Canning Street is to stand on the brink of possibility. The view to the city is clear, framed by sweet, 1880s Victorian terraces and tall 1930s palm trees that the looser corners of my imagination compare to a Californian boulevard. Laid out before you are the four corners of an inner northerner's world: Carlton, Fitzroy, the uni, the city.

To sit on a bike seat at the top of Canning Street is to feel like coming home. For morning commuters on two wheels, this is the point where the commute eases. Its back is broken: you've hustled across from the east or west, down cracked, narrow bike paths, dodging car doors, blind corners, pedestrian crossings. And now, you tilt into the easy bit. The broad, straight, uninterrupted swoop down to Princes Street on a perfectly angled decline. An inevitable pause where the bike highway meets the car highway; more coasting down to meet Elgin Street, where the free-wheeling horde is brought to a halt by a ponderous set of traffic lights and the ascent to Carlton Gardens.

(For a brief few months, perhaps only weeks, the council disastrously replaced the Pigdon Street roundabout with an intersection. I have never seen a piece of road infrastructure cause so much chaos. Cars and bikes both crept through the intersection – which still looked a *lot* like a roundabout

– in bewilderment, giving way to the right as they had always done, just in case other road users hadn't noticed the change. The roundabout was quickly reinstated, and despite the project being so ill-conceived in the first place, it was heartening to see the people's will get its way.)

I have been riding down Canning Street for the last eighteen years, on my way to uni, various jobs, parties, bars, pizza joints. (I never use it to get to the city; I'd rather take my chances with the Copenhagen lanes on Swanston Street than ride up that hill to Rathdowne.) And every time I still have that feeling – let's call it joy – as I enter the top of Canning Street and stop pedalling.

When I was a student, back when students could find places to live around Canning Street, we used to ride our bikes all over the place going to parties in share-houses in those sweet Victorian terraces. Canning Street itself was rarely a destination. Aside from the weirdly numerous corner wine shops that we could never afford to patronise, there was nothing to stop for. It was merely a conduit. We'd cycle boisterously into the night, spend a night shouting and drinking and talking, talking, talking about all the things we'd do with our lives, the things we'd fix in the world. The endless possibilities that are so apparent when you're standing at the top of your twenties and the view is clear and vast. And then we'd roll home – wobble, really – up Canning Street, or down; tipsy, but settling into those streets like a needle into its groove, our bikes almost steering themselves on the journey home.

It was a commonly held belief that you couldn't get done for drink-driving on a bike. We were all country kids, so though we didn't have cars, we all had our licences, and we didn't want to lose them. But a wise friend-of-a-friend with dreadlocks and an air of civil disobedience about him once told me that if you got spotted by the cops wobbling along Canning Street, or Drummond, or Amess, all you had to do was get off your bike and lift it into the air. He couldn't explain why. I supposed that somehow, it negated the bike's status as a "vehicle", or perhaps absolved you from the crime of driving a vehicle while over the limit, since you were instead merely carrying it.

Once, the police set up a booze bus in the Canning Street bike lane. On a Friday evening, just after work, just over the lights from the Dan O'Connell. I was a working, contributing member of society by that point, but as I cycled up to the check point, a mild panic tapped into my dormant student mind and drew out that piece of drunk-cycling lore. I slowed. Should I halt, dismount and carry my bike past? Should I alert my fellow commuters to this loophole?

Fortunately, my fellow commuters swarmed along unconcerned, and I had no time, and too much momentum, to stop and make a fool of myself. The cops waved some over beyond the witches' hats, but most of us kept on going, and I never had to test the lore.

I've since looked into it, and it appears the loophole is bullshit. I wonder what the wise man is doing now. The cops, for their part, were trying it on. In Victoria, they can't force cyclists to breath-test; and the worst they could have done us for is being "drunk in charge of a carriage", a law as old as the terrace houses, which no-one has seen fit to update in the 150 years since. My anxiety was unfounded anyway – I hadn't had so much as a pot of Carlton draft.

These days, Canning Street is busier in the mornings; the sheer mass of cyclists tips the traffic balance of power in their favour like nowhere else in Melbourne. It seems steeper in the evenings, as I struggle back to Brunswick with knees that are eighteen years older than they were. But it is still the groove to my needle. It still has a disproportionate number of corner wine shops, and there are still students there somewhere, who come out to loll on its median strip on summer evenings, basking in the sun, happily displaying their care-freedom to the world.

It is still broad and straight and full of possibility.

ON STATION STREET

Station Street, Carlton

JOHANNA ELLERSDORFER

I was tagged in a post on Facebook a few months ago by an old housemate I hadn't spoken to or seen for years. When I opened the message, I saw an ad for a freshly painted single storey Victorian terrace bereft of any character. It was flanked by an empty garden bed out the front and, I noticed as I scrolled down, a neatly paved backyard. Under the post was a string of names, including mine and those of my old housemates from the three years I spent on Station Street in Carlton North. Looking at the photos, I barely recognised it. It was sparse and neat and jarringly contemporary, filtered through the polarised lens of a real estate agent angling for a sale, and for a moment, I let myself wonder what had happened.

When I moved into that house on Station Street, it had been adorned with chipped ornaments and peeling beige paint, small patches entirely weathered away to reveal cross-sections of previous paint jobs and crumbling mortar. The front veranda was paved with loose terracotta tiles in what had once been a neat herringbone design, and a small garden was squeezed in between the veranda and slanted lacework fence, which had been painted white over layers of sanded-back paint, leaving dents and dimples in the surface. The garden was entirely overgrown with a single bushy tree that leaned wildly towards the landing, scratching at the red awning, and brushing the shoulders of anyone who walked through the creaking front gate.

Inside, the sagging foundations shifted palpably when we walked down the long hallway that ran from the front door, past all four bedrooms and the lounge room, and through to the dining room at the back of the house. Mysterious stains coloured the faded grey-green carpets, and illogically placed holes punctured the cream-coloured walls that must have once held hooks to display decorations in a way that made sense to the people who had lived there before us.

It had been a share house for decades and was full of mismatched furniture and items that no one claimed ownership of, but that invariably seemed to belong to the "house". It was as though this structure we inhabited was our fifth housemate, occasionally reminding us of its presence as the foundations groaned, and breaths of wind hissed down the defunct chimney recess in the dining room. There was a broken sofa in the lounge room disguised under an arrangement of carefully placed cushions, and in the tiny kitchen flimsy white cupboards were packed full of retro crockery webbed with dark cracks. Mismatched cups hung from hooks above the green-tiled bench and I often wondered where they had come from.

Soon after moving in, I began walking everywhere, eager to explore my new surrounds. I found a sense of purpose in navigating my way along routes I didn't know, using cross streets and compass directions to find my bearings. I came to recognise the palm trees on Canning Street, and discovered an allergy to the plane trees on Newry Street. I noticed that the terrace homes on Rathdowne Street were the largest and grandest, and I began to spot ghost signs painted on buildings, advertising Bushells tea and milk; their colours as faded and peeling as the paint on our house.

Compared to our house, Carlton North felt neat and organised. Its grid-like streets were lined with colourful terrace homes in varying states of repair, and even the parks were perfectly square, fitting neatly within the boundaries of the surrounding streets.

I decided at some point that it looked best at sunrise and sunset, like a Clarice Beckett painting shrouded in pink and mauve haze. Stubbornly, this is still how I remember it.

My room was initially a sublet, and for six months I lived among things that belonged to a girl I had never met. I slept on her futon, and used her large Ikea dining table as a desk, which I pushed away from the window and into a nook next to the fireplace in an attempt to make the room feel more like my own. In the mornings, I would be woken up by the unfamiliar sound of tram bells drifting over from Nicholson Street, and as winter crept in, drafts seeped through the gaps in ancient window frames that no longer sealed.

I felt as though I was an intruder in someone else's space, borrowing a life that was not mine, a charade as fragile as the tea cups that occasionally broke in the mornings, the ice cold porcelain shattering upon contact with boiled water when I made my morning tea. I have since lived in many other houses in many other cities, and I still wonder what it is that makes people feel so at home, so completely comfortable in a space, in which their existence must surely be temporary, fleeting even, because places just change so fast and nothing really lasts forever.

...

About a year into my time on Station Street, one housemate moved out and another moved in. At the request of our new housemate, we had the house cleared of spirits and bad energy. I remember referring to the woman who performed the clearing as the "spirit lady", but perhaps this wasn't a reference I shared out loud. She informed us that our house was situated on a crack in the universe and this was to blame for any sleeping problems. She also told me that a ghost was preventing me from finishing my thesis. This piece of information was strangely vindicating.

I felt the ghosts of past housemates in the large piles of unopened mail, addressed to people I had never met, but who had once inhabited this space and known it as intimately as I did. These envelopes would sit in the hallway, waiting for someone to decide whether to go to the effort of marking them each "return to sender" or to simply throw them away.

While I lived there, it never occurred to me to question why Station Street was called what it was. I never wondered if there had been a station, or where it might have been. Never wondered why it was no longer there. Years later I learnt that North Fitzroy station had once been at its northern end, where it is intersected by Park Street and the grid of Carlton North is ringed with the slender green strip of Linear Park. This is where the Inner Circle train line had once run and the station was indeed the namesake of the street. I suppose the ghosts of the suburb were lingering there too.

When you look at a map, Station Street is sliced in two by Princess Street at what is roughly its midpoint. Both halves of the street are slightly askew, as though they have been broken apart and stuck back together, imprecisely. Physically, this divide is also tangible, in the inconvenience of a pedestrian crossing and traffic barriers blocking cars from turning onto Station Street's southern end. On either side, it is flanked by bigger and busier streets that aren't hampered by this divide – Canning Street to the west and Nicholson Street to the east. By comparison, Station Street always felt like a quiet residential channel, floating between two thoroughfares.

Sometimes, as I roamed around the neighbourhood, I'd wander towards Canning Street, towards its long green median strips, planted with old palms and poplars and think that the grass actually was greener over there.

One of my housemates had a friend who lived in a share house on Canning Street. From his stories, it sounded like they were living in a protracted house party. I'd imagine them among the groups I'd see on warmer days, sitting casually on the median strip on blankets and scarves, eating makeshift picnic lunches and smoking cigarettes. These people seemed so much more cohesive than my own disconnected group of housemates and I envied how easily they seemed to inhabit space.

But there was a quietness to Station Street that I found comforting. If Canning Street was for extroverts, Station Street was for introverts. Instead of picnics on the median strip, it was a place to retreat. It was the safety of everyday existence, enacted alongside faceless neighbours in rows of matching terrace homes, behind lacework and wrought iron fences. It was suburbia in the inner city.

...

After about a year and a half in the house, I moved from my first bedroom, third along with a view out over the laneway, into the front room with a window opening out onto the street. I placed my desk right under the window, and as I worked, I would peek through the scraggly branches overgrown with foliage and see the neat line of pastel-coloured terrace homes across the road. It was surprising, although perhaps it shouldn't have been, to discover how little traffic passed by. I barely saw any walkers or cyclists and only really remember the occasional car, driving slowly along, perhaps looking for a place to park.

Unlike my first room, which had an old built-in wardrobe and a decorative fireplace, the front room was comparatively sparse. Front rooms in terrace homes were traditionally either the master bedroom or the parlour, a space used for receiving guests, and I am still unsure what this room might have been. Perhaps the ghost who was still doggedly preventing me from writing my thesis might have thought it a parlour and was simply invading my space, waiting patiently to be received.

One day in summer, not long after I'd moved into this room, the newest housemate, Tilly*, suggested sitting outside the front of our house. We carried two plastic folding chairs from the dining room and set them up on the footpath. Tilly was certain that we would meet interesting people, and strike up conversation with our neighbours as they wandered by. We sat uncomfortably for an hour or so, without seeing a single person, so we packed up our chairs and continued our conversation inside at the dining room table and never tried it again.

Despite our failed attempt at meeting the neighbours, I became friends with Tilly, and for the first time since I'd moved in, felt a small sense of companionship at home. I'm not sure how it started, but we soon began to refer to the house as the "halfway house". Once it had been articulated, it was impossible not to see. I was there, trying to finish my masters, working on a thesis that seemed to have stalled with an amorphous end date that never got any closer. Other housemates were there after leaving relationships, or biding their time before moving interstate or overseas. It was as though we were all in limbo and had been caught by this house that kept us safe, but also stopped us moving forward, trapping us in uncertainty until inevitably, we all somehow mustered the strength to move on.

The house had always had its quirks, and when rooms became available we often advertised this openly. The bathroom and kitchen were essentially the same room – separated by a flimsy door that didn't reach the ceiling meaning that the smell of cooking oil and shower gels regularly mingled in the back corner of the house – and the toilet was in the backyard. For this reason, a pair of communal gumboots was

*Name has been changed.

always kept at the backdoor. For most of the time I was there, there was no insulation, and in winter it was not uncommon to arrive home in the evening to a house that was colder inside than it was out. Until this point, I had found these features oddly charming, small quirks to be endured for the privilege of living in a place so beautifully old, but slowly they started to grate on me.

Outside, I also began to notice change. Increasingly, old run-down terraces like ours were being sold and renovated, emerging from behind construction boarding after a few months with slick paint jobs and perfectly manicured gardens. I could only imagine the kinds of renovations that went on inside, as walls were inevitably knocked down, carpets stripped, allowing airy, open-planned living spaces to emerge from the boxy Victorian floor plans that lent themselves so well to share housing. The demographic shifted too, as share houses packed up and families moved in, and the picnics on Canning Street moved further north towards Brunswick.

Somehow I finally finished my thesis and got a grant to spend some time overseas. I still had six months on Station Street, but I could see my end point and everything became coloured in the warm shades of nostalgia as I patiently waited to leave.

In those final months, I walked more and further than I had before. I would walk to work in Kew, snaking my way down Station Street and then over to Nicholson, before turning onto Johnson and walking straight along and up Studley Park Drive. I would walk north to East Brunswick, the houses spreading into stand-alone homes, Californian bungalows and fibro cottages with front and back gardens, but mostly I walked around Carlton North. It was as though I was filled with a sudden urgency to cement the physical memories of existing there, as though with leaving, my body might suddenly forget.

In my final weeks I slowly packed my belongings and sold what I could. My room became a shell of what it had been. A bed, a suitcase and some boxes, bereft of personality. The bare walls felt startlingly naked and the room felt devastatingly large, as though it had forgotten me already and had expanded in anticipation for the next person to pass through. The cool air of autumn began to seep in through the cracks and I knew it was time to leave. In the nine years since I have left Station Street, I have never lived anywhere as long as I lived in that house.

...

A few weeks ago, a colleague and I discovered we had both lived on Station Street. For a brief moment, we thought it might have been in the same house, our time on the street separated by a few years. As it turned out, she lived a block north, in a similar house, with overgrown bamboo in her front garden, not a scraggly tree. We sat with our phones out, looking at maps, pointing out to each other where we had walked, parks we had sat in, tram stops we'd used. "Did you like it there?" she asked suddenly, and I didn't know what to say. I had been surrounded by people and felt both suffocated and incredibly alone, but I loved that house for all its flaws, and all its ghosts.

I used to wonder which items of furniture might still be in use, which of the mugs had managed to survive another winter and if any mail addressed to me ever found its way into the letterbox. Perhaps it is still a share house, but I know this is unlikely. It was definitely sold, and by now it has probably been gutted entirely and renovated with skylights and open-plan living, like so many other homes in the area. But I remember it exactly as it was, in all its crumbling glory. I can still see those streets bathed in the soft pink light of summer sunsets and the clear mauve of long Melbourne twilights. Perhaps in some ways I am still there, a small trace of me forever in that house, as I remember roaming the streets of Carlton North.

MELBOURNE'S LITERARY STREETSCAPES

THUY ON

Melbourne's streets have been inspiring authors since the city was young. These are just some of the writers who exploit Melbourne's streets to give their stories an acute sense of place.

Fergus Hume – *The Mystery of a Hansom Cab*

Picture two men (one decidedly drunk) boarding a hansom cab in the early hours of the morning in Melbourne; a while later, the inebriated one is subsequently discovered dead, with a chloroform-soaked handkerchief tied over his mouth – the perpetrator having alighted earlier.

So begins Fergus Hume's *The Mystery of a Hansom Cab*, a best-selling crime novel of the nineteenth century and one that's never been out of print. Upon publication in 1886, the novel became a local and international blockbuster, with enviable sales figures that even Arthur Conan Doyle, Hume's authorial peer and rival at the time, couldn't match with his own debut, *A Study in Scarlet*.

English at birth, from a humble Scottish heritage (his father was a madhouse attendant), Hume was born at the Worcester County Pauper and Lunatic Asylum. The future author was raised in proximity to his father's troubled charges, a salutary education and useful upbringing for someone who would later write about crime. The family migrated to Dunedin, New Zealand, to take advantage of the goldrush-led prosperity there, before twenty-five-year-old Hume departed for boom-time Melbourne, Australia's entertainment capital, to further his playwriting ambitions.

The Mystery of a Hansom Cab was written as a vehicle to attract those in the theatrical world. Though he had a law degree, Hume fancied himself as a bohemian and was far more interested in cultivating the artistic muse. Research led him to write a detective thriller, cannily incorporating the local colour into his novel to appeal to the market. His taste for melodrama, flair for dramatic dialogue and legal background made a potent brew.

The streetscapes of Melbourne's CBD and her suburbs play a significant role in the plot of *The Mystery of a Hansom Cab*, and though writing at a time when the city was a bustling, wealthy metropolis, Hume explores the social class divide throughout his novel. Today you can still trace the route of the hansom cab from the corner of Collins and Russell streets, along the boulevard to St Kilda. References to local streets, laneways and landmarks reveal how Hume understood the importance of place in detective fiction; how the setting can influence the crime.

Geoffrey Blainey wrote in *A History of Victoria* that *The Mystery of a Hansom Cab* "did more than any book to give the outside world a picture of Melbourne of the late 1880s". Indeed in its first English edition, the book was advertised as "a startling and realistic story of Melbourne social life."

Diligent in his research, Hume claims that "All the scenes in the book, especially the slums, are described from personal observation; and I passed a great many nights in Little Bourke Street, gathering material." From mansions to opium dens, his extremes of rich and poor are best represented by the Collins Street block and the slums of Little Bourke Street (which are a stone's throw from one another). He contrives a plot that brings their separate worlds together. It's also a story about people shedding their past and reinventing themselves by coming to a new country, the eternal plight of the immigrant. The book includes notable features of the colonial city that are still in existence: Scotch Church, the Yarra River, Chinatown, the Melbourne Club, Town Hall, Treasury and Fitzroy gardens, St Kilda's pier and esplanade.

The book is written with gritty realism and an ear for the vernacular, and a number of Hume's characters have a touch of Dickensian grotesqueness about them (the aptly named Mother Guttersnipe for instance). Here is his description of Collins Street on a fashionable Saturday morning: "As the sun brings out bright flowers so the seductive influence of the hot weather had brought out all the ladies in gay dresses of innumerable colours, which made the long street look like a restless rainbow. Carriages were bowling smoothly along, their occupants smiling and bowing as they recognised their friends on the sidewalk; lawyers, their legal quibbles finished for the week, were strolling leisurely along, with their black bags in their hands; portly merchants, forgetting Flinders Lane and incoming ships, were walking beside their pretty daughters, and the representatives of swelldom were stalking along in their customary apparel of curly hats, high collars, and masher suits ..."

Contrast this dazzling scene of moneyed power to the narrow grimness of Little Bourke Street, with its "high buildings on each side, the dim light of the sparsely scattered gas lamps, and the few ragged looking figures slouching along ... on the one side a man cowering back into the black shadow ... on the other a woman with disordered hair and bare bosom, leaning out of a window trying to get a breath of fresh air." Hume wrote a tale that depended upon the unexpected collision of the worlds of the honorable and dishonorable; of heiresses and millionaires, prostitutes, gamblers and drunkards.

Aside from numerous play and film adaptations of the novel, there has also been an 1888 parody, *The Mystery of a Wheel-Barrow*.

Unfortunately, having sold the rights to *The Mystery of a Hansom Cab* for fifty pounds, the author and aspiring but failed playwright never profited from its phenomenal success, and his subsequent 100-plus novels and short stories never received the same positive critical reception. He died in relative obscurity in England in 1932.

Nonetheless, the continuing popularity of Hume's novel and the care with which he mapped out the streets of this crime fiction ensures that *The Mystery of a Hansom Cab* remains an important landmark in Melbourne's literary history.

Meg Mundell – *Black Glass*

Meg Mundell's *Black Glass* offers a speculative near-future dystopia; although its setting uses real-life locations, it does not pretend to paint a realist picture. Instead it's Melbourne's CBD in a parallel universe that nonetheless deals with very real, contemporary problems. The very title *Black Glass* has several connotations: the city seen through a dark lens (through a glass darkly), a shadowy future that threatens to come into focus if we take the wrong path and the dark lens of surveillance (a technology that controls and divides our cities). In the book, an imagined future is superimposed on present-day Melbourne and acts as a warning that this is how things will eventuate if we don't take due care of our world and of each other.

Despite its grimness, the story is imbued with hope: it's about friendship, courage and survival amongst people living on the margins of society. Mundell's debut novel is also a fictionalised account of voices we never hear much from in fiction: members of the homeless community. Mundell reminds us they are citizens with rights and histories too. It's a busy, energetic book populated by a motley cast of characters: street kids, muck-racking journalists, predators and manipulators. *Black Glass* roams widely throughout Melbourne's streets: from specific locations such as the Docklands, the Star Wheel and Southern Cross and Flinders Street stations, the casino and the NGV fountain, to alleyways, rooming houses, nightclubs and city towers. Teenage sisters Grace and Tally are the main protagonists, who become separated in this crumbling urban world. They are "undocs", without proper documentation to validate their existence, and like the other undocs, left to fend for themselves.

The contrast between romanticised hope and ominous reality is shown in sharp relief. On entering Melbourne from the Hume Highway on the outskirts of the CBD, this is Tally's first vision of the city: "It soared up against the morning sky just like Tally had imagined: every dream of a city, every TV show and magazine ad. Light leaked in from a low angle and the skin of the buildings shone, rectangle upon rectangle, pink air repeated in a hundred thousand mirrors."

But as she draws closer to her destination, "Tally saw that a brown haze hovered over the city, like a thick smudge of cigar smoke." Melbourne is rendered as apocalyptic, run to seed because of climate change, pollution and profiteering. The Yarra River "was choked with plastic bottles and old coupons; its tea-brown depths merged with the oily harbour of the Docklands, where vacant high-rise towers and basement strip joints marked the dodgy part of town. Most of the fountains in the city grid were dry now, just drifting spots for dead leaves and fast-food litter."

Contemporary Melbourne is still recognisable in this cautionary tale where the divide between the haves and the have-nots has become a chasm. But there is also a bright, carnivalesque element with The Quarter, a lawless zone where hustlers, bohemians and entertainers mingle, party and earn a living. Mundell also inserts a note of fantasy in her creation of a "moodie", who manipulates crowds by altering the sensory environment. Let loose at various concerts, clubs, sporting stadiums and casinos to ply his craft, this figure of surveillance, control and profit is responsible for changing public temperament by changing the lights, temperature, music and scents. That the media also plays a cynical role in manipulating minds is another a thematic concern.

The narrative is told via a number of stylistic devices, which brings to mind a state-kept dossier on individual activity: there are notebook entries, news snippets, email exchanges, transcribed conversations, and descriptions of CCTV footage among the mix. These broken up scenes add to the feeling of a divided, disjointed world.

Though ostensibly set in Melbourne's CBD, in a sense *Black Glass* is about the potential dark futures of all Western cities, a possible tomorrow ruled by a draconian Big Brother government, with depleted natural resources (there is a lack of clean drinking water) and an underclass of scrabblers.

Kerry Greenwood – *Ruddy Gore*
Rebecca Lim – *The Astrologer's Daughter*

Welcome to Little Bourke Street: "chilly, empty and dark. Sodium glare from the widely spaced street lights turned every puddle on the slick cobbles into a mirror and let black velvet pools of night in between." This ominous setting opens Kerry Greenwood's *Ruddy Gore*, her seventh in the Phryne Fisher series, which begins in Chinatown, Little Bourke Street, and moves to Her Majesty's Theatre, where Phryne is waiting with her companion Bunji Ross to see a performance of Gilbert and Sullivan's *Ruddigore*.

Kerry Greenwood's twenty Fisher novels feature the black-bobbed, impeccably attired, accidental detective in a series of capers set in and around Melbourne in the twenties. Sassy, brainy, independently wealthy and with a canny sense for adventure, Phryne adds a glamorous touch to crime fiction, a genre that can often be dour and grimy. Greenwood's series is especially created for those who like their murder mysteries frothy rather than forensic. As a liberal sophisticate and proto-feminist, her sleuth is a refreshing counterpoint to the grouchy old male gumshoe. Extensively researched, Greenwood's books are historical dramas in themselves, a repository for all sorts of details about life in the bustling interwar period.

Phryne has a "roll in the gutters" in Little Bourke St when she saves an elderly Chinese woman by hitting the woman's assailants with the back of a hatchet. (Our heroine was "clad in an outrageously expensive dress and didn't want to get blood on it".) She earns the gratitude of the matriarch's grandson Lin Chung, a local silk merchant, and later becomes involved in his family's feuding dramas. Fortunately this street altercation does not change her evening plans, and Phryne soon joins the rest of Melbourne society gathered at Her Majesty's to see the gala show. The theatre was "ablaze with light … Expensive cars were stopping to allow expensive by-invitation-only patrons to alight. There was a scent of French perfume so strong, as to be almost a stench, and a flurry of coats, cloaks and glossy top hats."

It's at the theatre where Phryne finds her newest case, when during the performance of the operetta, two of its leading actors are poisoned, a prompter is murdered and even a ghost is seen a-haunting the floorboards. The narrative cleverly creates links between the Chinese community in Little Bourke St, the outlandish comic plot of the Gilbert and Sullivan show, and the acting troupe at Her Majesty's. Of course, like in all her other books, Phryne coasts through the dangers with a jaunty spring in her step and nary a hair out of place.

To Greenwood's credit, *Ruddy Gore* is not all about the antics of the flashy, dissembling thespians; through Lin Chung the reader also learns a little bit about the difficulty of integrating into Australian culture from an outsider's perspective. One should be reminded though, that this book is set in 1928, so racist beliefs and descriptions of the Chinese were commonplace. Walking along with him, Phryne notices that "altogether, Little Bourke Street was as interesting and bustling as Shanghai, with the same bamboo washing poles which bannered laundry above the street, fewer sing-song girls and the same strange scents."

Greenwood's descriptions are sensuous and evocative. This particular enclave of Chinatown "was narrow and crowded … the air smelt overwhelmingly of fruit, with an underscent of saffron, garlic, dust, people and motor exhaust … Little shops with tiny windows breathed forth a smell of herbs and strange spices. Each one appeared to be staffed by an old woman in dark trousers and tunic, her head wrapped in a white scarf, with an attendant cat sitting at her feet". (Says Chung, every shop has this "small tiger" to ward off rats and demons.)

In *The Astrologer's Daughter*, Rebecca Lim also writes of Little Bourke Street, with its ceremonial stone gateway "between a pair of snarling stone lions with curved fangs, bulbous eyes and clawed feet", and the female restaurant touts at night time, with "their slinky, faux silk cheongsams and Uggs, waving menus at anything living that goes by." With its collision of past, present and future, and its firm setting of place, the book also offers a gateway into Melbourne's seedy underside. Written in 2014, this contemporary young-adult coming-of-age fiction is also partially set in and around the painted arches of Melbourne's Chinatown.

With her mother, eighteen-year-old Avicenna lives on the top floor of a three-storey Victorian-era brick building in the heart of Chinatown, with the pungent scent of the XO sauce of the restaurant wafting through from next door. But when Joanne goes missing, Avicenna, who's inherited her gift for reading the stars, has to revisit a cold case to make sense of her mother's disappearance.

Lim is the author of nineteen books for children and YA readers, but straddling between realism and mysticism, *The Astrologer's Daughter* defies easy categorisation. The book interweaves themes of parental and romantic love, gender-based violence, spirituality, fate and determinism. It's a beguiling genre-bender, a paranormal thriller couched within the typical parameters of teenage life. Lim fully exploits the distinctly Melbourne CBD streets in her novel, with its mentions of trams, the St Kilda Road police complex, Flagstaff Gardens, Russell, Elizabeth, Exhibition and Little Latrobe streets, Her Majesty's Theatre and the Chinese Museum.

TRIUMPH
HONDA
all
MODELS
PH. 67-5356

LIKE MORTAR

Degraves Street, Melbourne

ANNA KATE BLAIR

I feel, in Degraves Street, as if I am a tourist on a ghost tour. I left Melbourne nine years ago and grew up, I thought, but I've tumbled back into adolescent melodrama upon return. I'm afraid of my ghosts materialising; I am afraid because I know that they are not ghosts, really, but people who walk the streets, haunting but alive.

This is where people bubble up into the city; surface, ascend from underground. I have questions about the history of this laneway, which was named for the owners of a flour mill in the nineteenth century, and transformed by the Degraves Street Subway in 1955. The underpass is tiled in candy pink, with black granite columns and worn doors, wooden and often locked, signs saying *Telephones* and display windows in which creatures from artists' fantasies live, brightly lit. I love this underpass, which connects Flinders Street Station with Degraves Street. It smells, at the threshold, like waffles.

...

I wasn't a tourist, as an undergraduate, and yet I spent so much time on Degraves Street, which is listed in every traveller's guidebook. It was close to the railway station; it was reliable. It was a place to meet when time was limited, or it was a way in which to slip into the city, quietly, without the clamour of Swanston Street, without the rush of trams.

...

I keep thinking of one of the tables at the back of Degraves Espresso. I remember them as oriented in another direction; I don't know if they've been rearranged or if it's my memory that's at fault. I remember that I tried to have breakfast there once, a decade ago, with an on-off lover, almost gone. He had told me, one week earlier, that he had decided to date my friend. I had decided not to eat. He wanted me to be ok; healthy, strong. Starvation was the only form of revenge that I could muster.

Eat, he said, and bought me pancakes.

I'll have the strawberry, I said, and nibbled at the garnish.

He cut up the pancakes for me, as if I were his child, and sat with me as I cried, for hours, and rain fell beyond his shoulders, beyond the café window, making our table cosy and the world outside grey. I can't remember what happened afterwards, which of us walked toward the station and which of us walked instead through Centre Place to Collins Street, or perhaps along Flinders Lane, but I know that we parted and that was that, that was finished, except that it wasn't, because Melbourne is a city in which eyes always meet in laneways and nobody can be avoided forever. We are arranged within a grid; we intersect.

...

I had to sell or give away, upon returning, all the clothes that I had kept in storage.

"We can't take this," said the woman at the consignment store. "It's too small. None of our customers will fit this."

I don't remember being thin, though. I just remember that strawberry garnish, those pancakes, and eating only when he was kind to me, in Degraves Espresso. I remember coffee, wine, the endless repetition of certain streets.

"I like you, but I don't like you enough," he said the first evening, holding my hand.

"Enough for what?" I asked, kept asking.

. . .

I am not sure really if the Degraves Street Subway should be seen as a continuation of the street or a ghostly double, an underground echo. I am not sure, either, about the point at which love affairs cease to be real, inhabited, and become myth, places from the past to be feared.

. . .

I was asked by an acquaintance, soon after we met, if I had kissed him.

"Not yet," I said, without thinking.

It felt preordained, instinctive. I just waited and, eventually, something happened.

. . .

I am afraid of running into him and yet I am not afraid that he will read this essay. Why, I wonder, is the street more frightening than the page? It is, I suppose, the ways in which we brush against one another, surprise one another, wrestle with power; in a laneway, I do not know which of us will have somewhere else to be.

I remember when I was a teenager in the suburbs, when everybody I knew went to Chadstone Shopping Centre to buy jeans or see films or just to loiter with a milkshake. I was anonymous then in the city. I am nostalgic for the age when nobody I knew caught public transport or drank coffee in laneways, for the years in which I lived in Melbourne without naming Degraves Street. It is a nostalgia that is premised upon love; I want the city emptied so that I might fill it only with those who I want to see, and with strangers, so that I might wander freely, unafraid, untethered, as if a tourist.

. . .

I feel certain that he was telling the truth when he said that he loved me, one night over the telephone, even as he told me the next day on a platform at Flinders Street Station, after we'd finished our coffee and left Degraves Street, two years or so before the pancakes, that he regretted saying it. I was nineteen years old and motherless, full of grief, untethered from my suburban past and unsure about my future. I was too distressed for a nineteen-year-old boy to handle, even as he kissed me and unbuttoned my dresses and told me that we were not dating, that we needed to stop doing whatever it was that we were doing.

"He was a dickhead," my friends say, now.

"We were just young," I say, and hate that this city makes me feel proximate to that youth.

...

"I think it's good you're leaving," said a friend when I was accepted to graduate school, in the United Kingdom.

...

I remember scratches on my hand from being pushed and kissed against walls, in that spot where there is a void between the laneway's buildings. The walls are still here, still rough, but covered by different street art. I was such a child. I feel embarrassed by the contours of the laneway, by how little they have changed, by the smell of waffles close to the dumpsters. I think of the past as sandwiched between the bricks, like mortar; it has been painted over, but not demolished.

...

"I think it's really good you're leaving," said another friend, four years later, when that lost lover moved to the UK after me, following me to the same town, the same university, the same residential college, and I took a fellowship in France.

I was seeking, I know now, a kind of obliteration through desire. I've had it explained since that I am drawn to difficult relationships by my mother's death, by the need for fresh bodies to cry over, but I did not know then why I was so addicted to somebody who hurt me, repeatedly, by always leaving. I stayed away from South Yarra, from the hospital in which my mother died and the vast expanse of green that sits across from it, unprotected, but the city's sunless laneways are just an inversion, perhaps; there's no escaping one's own patterns.

...

I am back in Melbourne now, and nobody has said that that's a good thing. I am afraid, sometimes, to leave my flat. I have begun to wear mascara again, after years of doing otherwise. I shouldn't care, as it was years ago, but I am afraid that time is like the city grid, that I can't help but end up in the same places.

...

I used to wander through the city with the friend he started dating, in the years before that happened. There was a lingerie shop then in Degraves Street that we used to visit together. We both liked lace and pastel colours and owned many of the same undergarments. I wondered, later, if he recognised her bras.

I saw that former friend's mother once later, in another laneway. I was sitting with a friend, drinking coffee, and she was walking briskly. She looked at me, but made no acknowledgement of our acquaintance; she kept her mouth in a tight line, unsmiling.

...

I try now to listen to the sounds in Degraves Street. I hear the clink of cafes closing; it is late at night. It is raining. There is a hardness to the heavy drops hitting the umbrellas at the centre of the lane; it reminds me of poured gravel or electronic interference. I find it peaceful; I feel far from youth.

...

I remember more than unrequited love, of course. I remember my best friend's legs, in tights that placed a stylised eye on each knee, one winking, as she stood on the corner of Degraves Street and Flinders Lane, waiting for me. I remember coffees, dinners, smiles and laughter, eating outdoors without a coat in winter, chilly, introducing Grill'd to a tourist who was unimpressed, but all these memories are background chatter; it is the moments that provoke the strongest feelings that are remembered clearly, and my strongest sensation was that of being hurt.

I remember walking through a series of laneways and arcades to avoid the trams, which seemed slower then, and to avoid the crush of crowds on Swanston Street. Everybody it seems was doing this, and we all ran into one another, often. It's hard to believe that we darted through the city, on foot, to save time. We may have done this simply so that we could feel the city in our bodies, meld with it, shape our legs as we stepped into it, so that we could construct ourselves through the laneways, map our university days onto spaces in which we did not study.

...

I am trying now to meet the gaze of my younger self, that ghost. I want to tell her of all the things that she is missing out on, suggest that she sleep with other people. Did I mention that he was Catholic? It was, for me, for her, an education in yearning. I want to suggest that this girl go to therapy, start taking antidepressants, though I know that she was told that, then, and sometimes in this laneway, and that she didn't listen, that she was afraid of life and its major thoroughfares, was looking for sheltered spaces, for somebody to protect her, for a mother, to travel backward in time.

...

I keep wanting to write in third person; I slip into it, scroll back, edit it out. It is difficult to believe that this girl was me. I have another body now, formed by other cities, through eating more and loving less. I still feel stabs of pain and recognition, though; I cringe at her behaviour even as I sympathise.

I struggle to write about Melbourne, about this lost lover and lost friend. I wonder now if I could move across this psychological block as I move across a city block, negotiating comfort and unease, slipping into shops and stopping to look for traffic, but rarely staying still, letting things stagnate. I could approach the past from an angle, obliquely, stepping delicately up into it as if from the Degraves Street Subway, finding places to linger as I cross space, cross time. I wonder, now, if any chance encounter would feel fine.

A LIFETIME OF LOVE

Swanston Street, Melbourne

JOHN WHITE

"'Shit, it's the police!"

We had just left a "drink-a-thon" at Melbourne University, at the far end of my favourite street, Swanston Street. Due to a tram strike (a common scenario in the seventies) we had boarded my brother's yellow Renault 10 to take us home. Due to the one-dollar unlimited beer, we were very drunk.

I fumbled out from the back seat and spread my legs wide apart with my hands stretched out on the roof, ready to be frisked then cuffed.

The policeman spoke firmly. There could be no reply.

"Driver, you were driving without your lights on. Lock the car up, and if you move it from this place before sunrise you will get a ticket."

The car spent the night half way down Swanston Street just outside the Town Hall, and no crime was recorded against the driver.

Swanston Street is Melbourne's C*ardo Maximus*, the most important north–south street found in any large Roman city. Integral to a city's plan, it is the hinge or axis of the city, but the meaning derives from the Greek for *heart*, and as such it is the hub of any city's economic life, filled with shops and vendors.

In 1837, Swanston Street was imposed on the bush and the dismayed

Indigenous people, appearing as part of the grid plan that was to become Melbourne. It was named after one of the Tasmanian financiers of the scheme, Charles Swanston.

Swanston Street begins at the entrance to the city with Princes Bridge, which has stretched across the Yarra River since 1888; prior to this was the wooden bridge in 1840, and between those two, the stone Lennox Bridge of 1851. It faithfully brought in travellers, trade and customers from St Kilda Road, via horses, carts then cars and later a huge number of trams, making it the busiest tramway in the world.

Moving north, on the left-hand side is Flinders Street Station, Australia's first city railway station, its entrance peppered with clocks that rarely work, but were intended to let you know when the next train was leaving for each line. "Meet you under the clocks", is still a favourite catch phrase. There are always plenty of weirdos hanging about there, so why not arrange to meet your friends there too.

My school had cadets, and we were issued with bolt-action guns. To get home we would take a tram to Flinders Street Station. Groups of ten boys with guns are rarely seen these days on public transport.

The trains flood thousands into the city every day from the surrounding suburbs, aided since the early 1980s by an underground rail loop. On New Year's Eve, Swanston Street gets so full of people streaming into the city to watch the fireworks that it is pointless to attempt walking. Instead, allow the crowd to sweep you to wherever it wants to take you. It may simply take you across Swanston Street to Federation Square, once occupied by two ugly Gas and Fuel skyscrapers and railway lines streaming from the station. Now there is an enormous digital screen where world events are enjoyed in the open by groups of strangers who come together to share a sporting match or concert or just the night air. Watching TV at home is no longer enough; besides, there are many trendy cafes and restaurants in the square.

The yearly Anzac Parade remembers those we lost at war protecting our existence, while Moomba celebrates that existence. Moomba, held each autumn with a parade up Swanston Street, was created four years after a "Fifty years of Federation" parade, and it remains Australia's largest free community festival. At first criticised as hedonistic and embodying social decay, it has been tidied up with imaginative floats, marching groups, the crowning of monarchs, fireworks, birdman competitions and bands amid the carnivals along the Yarra. Not at all hedonistic.

Just as Roman cities have a temple as you enter the city, we have ours: St Paul's Cathedral, on the corner of Swanston and Flinders. Melbourne's first public Christian services were held on this site in 1836. They shared the site with a corn market until 1852, when, finally, the bluestone St Paul's Parish Church emerged, and there the following year my great-great-grandfather married his love. He was an Irish sea captain, and she, a descendant of Protestant Palatine German refugees that had settled in Ireland, escaping the Great Famine. You can't see the old church, for it was replaced in 1886 by the new cathedral, which today has a big welcome sign up for refugees. This would have pleased my great-great grandparents.

Opposite the cathedral and the station is a pub built over the site where John Batman built a home for his children. This house later became a schoolhouse, then a warehouse, and in 1861 the Princes Bridge Hotel. In 1875, two Irishmen took it over: Young and Jackson. The pub holds a fine portrait of a naked lady, "Chloe", whose real name was Marie, a nineteen-year-old stunner immortalised by French painter Jules Lefebvre. It is just as well he did, for she committed suicide two years later after a failed love affair. She lives on here, loved by thousands.

Going up Swanston Street, on the left used to be eateries filled with personalities selling thin, hard, overcooked steaks with soggy chips and the significant one piece of lettuce, referred to as the "salad". All gone, replaced now with MacDonald's, Hungry Jacks, KFC, 7-11 and overseas-made Australian souvenir shops, among other less personal shops. I don't know their names any more and they don't recognise me; the personalities have gone, but then I have aged, while the staff seem to stay young.

The Nicholas Building, built by my neighbours' ancestors, is like a part of Chicago from the early 1920s. This little beehive has shops that specialise in fine French stitchery, books, eclectic collections; it's a private place for "those in the know". The lifts, once the oldest operating manual lifts in the city, have only recently lost their operator, who had carefully decorated the small working place as a reflection of home.

Dammon's Tobacconist, established in 1854, stood on the corner of Swanston and Collins Street. My younger brother worked there for a time and learnt that the secret of selling pipes was to match the length of the pipe to the height of the person. There are no Freudian connotations here, just good sales technique. It is now replaced by Westpac bank; I doubt these things are considered when applying for bank loans.

Slipping into a small arcade beside the Westpac bank is OM, the vegetarian Indian café where a small fee will get you all you can eat and much more: for their mission is "sharing love, inner peace and a vegetarian lifestyle," and it is true. How we would have loved OM to be there after school rowing on the Yarra each Saturday, for there was nowhere to buy food. The shops in the city closed at noon on Saturdays until 1987, and it took a decade more before Sunday trading began. There was one hamburger shop in Swanston Street. Filled with Laminex chrome tables, each embraced by a built-in couch. The Italian owner looked forward to us coming to fill his shop and gave us all a good feed.

Once in what is currently the city square, in front of the Westin Hotel, was Drews leather and travel goods shop. Sitting at the Swanston

Street entrance to Queen's Walk, which ran around the back of the Town Hall Hotel, Drews was renowned for its specialised goods. Here Grandma bought her leather hat boxes and handbags. She fortunately was not there when in 1950 a gas explosion collapsed the three-storey Town Hall Hotel. The city's largest explosion damaged Drews along with seventeen other buildings, and shattered 400 windows. No-one died, and grandma continued to buy at Drews.

The state of Victoria was officially established in 1851, and Melbourne, being its largest city, needed a large town hall, which was built in Swanston Street at the Collins Street intersection. This was rebuilt in the 1870s in the Second Empire style, and then again after a fire in 1925. (My great uncle was Lord Mayor in the early 1950s and has been credited with securing the Olympic Games for Melbourne in 1956.)

When the Beatles emerged from the city's reception at the Town Hall in 1964, I was among the thousands to greet them. I also loved attending the prom concerts held at the town hall, where a pillow, rug and space on the floor allowed a bohemian attitude to prevail instead of the snobbery usually associated with classical music. Proms are still going, but for me getting off the floor would be a challenge.

Across Swanston Street from the Town Hall is an elegant building, dressed in Art Deco attire, as if waiting to be invited to a ball. The Manchester Unity Independent Order of Oddfellows built this beauty in 1931. My dentist worked there for some years, and so I have mixed feelings about it once past the fine exterior. The memory of his drill turning slowly with its long pulleys and no water jet, years before the modern air turbine drills became common, still gives me discomfort.

Next along on the left is the Capitol Theatre, opened 1924 having been designed by Walter Burley Griffin, designer of the city of Canberra. It is now part of RMIT. Its huge geometric plaster ceiling was once filled with The Sound of Music, my daughter being one of the many cult fans who held a twig of edelweiss and sang along with the film and no-one minded.

The Chinese have been in Melbourne since the gold rush days and created a Chinatown, which now extends well beyond the arch that once confined it. Chinese cuisine has exploded onto Swanston Street, especially at the twenty-year-old QV centre. The QV centre wraps around what was once the Queen Victoria Hospital for women, on the site of Melbourne's first hospital, built in the 1850s.

The Greek shops in Swanston Street have closed, along with the Greek cultural centre in the Curtin building. Today Curtin House is filled with modern restaurants and bars. The building has experienced a full life, from the classics, to being the headquarters of the Communist Party of Australia, and now as home to the capitalists.

So many large public buildings appeared in the 1850s following the gold rush in Victoria, which brought in thousands with their money and a strong civic pride. The State Library of Victoria, found behind the pigeons, sculptures and picnickers, was one of these buildings. Since 1854 it has made its mark as Australia's oldest public library, a pioneer in the world for free libraries. A section was given to become the Museum of Melbourne, filled with a sampling of the world's treasures. These include the massive racehorse Phar Lap, a great New Zealand horse who lifted the spirits of many in the Great Depression of the 1930s, but then died unexpectedly. Perhaps poisoned or simply from an infection. My great-great-great uncle brought a man-sized painting out from England and displayed it in the museum for two weeks. He was given the sixteenth-century painting in lieu of payment for work done. *Christ at the Column*, by Guido Reni, was exhibited in 1876, but today it is in the National Gallery of Victoria storerooms: although accolades flew in all directions at the time, my uncle never lived to find out it is now considered a fake.

Further north are the older RMIT buildings; near here the Romans would have placed a public bath, and indeed this is where the City Baths are. I learnt to swim here, with my grandmother putting bathers on to join me in the water while a lady held a large stick with a hoop around my waist from the edge of the pool. On the corner with Victoria Street, Grandma's Norwegian father had a large grocery shop, selling supplies to the Carlton United Brewery opposite. Beer was brewed here from 1858, the brewery expanding to a huge block until finally moving out of the city in 1987. The workers could often be found noisy and drunk at lunchtime, as CUB provided them with free beer during lunch. No occupational health concerns then. Today it is the RMIT design hub.

There were many wonderful bookshops in Swanston Street, but a favourite of mine was The Scientific and Technical Bookshop at 295, which occupied two stores and provided books on any subject remotely related to science. Selby's Chemicals further along at 393 provided a huge range of scientific instruments, glassware and chemicals. I had read a "How and Why" book that revealed the components needed to make gunpowder. At Selby's I was able to buy two ingredients, but they would not sell me the potassium nitrate (saltpetre), as I was in school uniform. I needed this key ingredient to make an explosion. It was easy to convince my mother to buy the elusive component, as it was *needed* for my *experiments* with the chemistry set given to me for Christmas. She came home with a kilogram. I was not in possession of it for long, however, packing a test tube tightly with the correct proportions and blowing up a small part of the footpath outside our house; the rest was confiscated by irate parents. A visit from the federal police would surely follow today.

As a medical student I spent many sleepless nights at the Royal Women's Hospital, located then where the Dental Hospital is now, waiting to deliver babies. In the 1970s a medical graduate needed to deliver twenty babies before qualifying. We would sleep in the rooms provided, waiting for the huge bell over the door to ring when an expectant mother came into labour. Once we delivered a child, our name would go to the bottom of the list and so we could escape from the hospital without being missed. We shared these deliveries with the trainee midwives. Once, with my foot in plaster and using crutches, I raced to a delivery ward, delivered the first twin successfully and was pushed aside as a keen midwife moved into place for the second twin; there were no exceptions. Today's medical students are not required to have delivered any babies to graduate.

Living at the university it was common for me to walk to the city down Swanston Street. Several times large groups of people holding up signs and shouting joined me. In 1970, one hundred thousand came with me and gathered in Collins Street for the city's largest peace rally. The war in Vietnam ended five years later.

Instead of walking *down* the street, simply walking *across* Swanston Street created an awesome mental transformation. Libraries, lecture halls and essay writing were left behind and in nearby Lygon Street, I entered Little Italy to be spoilt with food and bookshops.

Don't forget Madeline. Until 1925 the far end of Swanston Street near the Melbourne Cemetery was called Madeline Street, and here can be found one of the thinnest houses in Melbourne, only one room wide. I enjoyed dinner one night with the owner, who loved and hated the house, and he was thinner than me.

In the 1990s, private traffic was blocked from Swanston Street, and now only bikes, trams and pedestrians take the journey. The other day I turned the car left up into Swanston Street from Collins Street, for a moment forgetting my street was no longer mine. A young policeman's severe stare and directive arm turned me around and I sulked back down the street. He knew nothing of my first interaction with the law here, racing down the empty tram tracks careless and free, fifty years ago, with my brother at the wheel. He knew nothing of my love for all its buildings and their stories. I realised then I will need to share my street with future generations, something each lifetime has found in the last 180 years, so they too can have a love affair with our sturdy, persistent friend.

So, what more can I say about a street that has provided civic pride, bomb-making chemicals, bookshops, music performances, a treasure of a museum, a transport hub, the joy of academia and that of delivering babies, amid so many other adventures? A street that has welcomed all nations to our emporium city, directing them northwards out into Victoria, while offering them reasons to stay. This is not a street, this is a lifetime of love; it is the lifeline of Melbourne.

South

LEARNING THE ROPES

Acland Street, St Kilda

ARATHI SRIPRAKASH

I set off on my bike from Brunswick at dawn – down Lygon, Swanston, then crossing the tangle of tram tracks on St Kilda Road. Smugness turned the pedals: I rolled down these traffic-free streets before most rolled out of bed. (I was yet to know about the early morning routine of parents, or anyone outside the eighteen to twenty-one-year-old age bracket). But really, it was the satisfaction that I would save myself the tram fare or, more honestly, the anxious dance of the fare-evader (stay near the doors, never make eye-contact). The recently installed plain-clothed ticket-checkers meant you could trust no one.

It was early December and already hot. I started my Sunday morning shifts on Acland Street with a sheen that did not look out of place next to the steaming coffee-machine. The café was new to me. I had crossed the river and now knew that artichoke could go on toast and that people were very serious about soy dandies. Mind you, the beards on today's hipsters had not yet sprouted. It was 2001, before irony broke the banks of the Yarra.

I was lucky to get the job. A friend had put in a good word, and now I worked cash-in-hand-with-a-few-sneaky-pastries-on-the-side. When I went for the interview, I walked along Acland to try to fill myself in it, this new side of town. Old ladies and druggies, artists and entrepreneurs. So many places for one to get cake. Everyone was in black and I was absurdly dressed in my Job Interview Clothes: a beige pencil-skirt and teal blouse.

I celebrated getting my new gig by buying an eye-liner pencil from the pharmacy down the road and a florentine from the rival café next door. Then I went to meet my also-new boyfriend down at the beach. Over a decade later and a continent away, I still wear black eye-liner and, as it turns out, mostly black everything else. The boyfriend also stayed. Melbourne has a way of hanging on to you.

My accomplice behind the counter was Corrine. She was a real local, unlike me – an interloper from up north. She was confident and smart and friendly. A Good Person. She showed me the ropes of the café and told me about streets and schools I'd never heard of this side of the river. Through her, I studied how to fit in. We bantered during quiet times and moved skilfully around each other during busy times. We'd often spend a little too long rearranging the bread in the front window so that we could watch people in the street. On hot days we'd linger in the cold store for as long as possible. We were friends of sorts, but we never saw each other outside the café.

Corrine and I would greet the regulars of Acland Street as if they were our friends but I knew nothing of their lives. I suspected they were different to me, but not too many years later I would find myself stepping with ease through worlds that I assume were similar to theirs. Secure work, dinner parties, and tofu in pumpkin soup. By chance, and long after my gig at the café ended, I read a book that had been written by one of our regulars. In it, she thanked the "great coffee" and "convivial vibe" of Acland Street that had helped her to write. Of course, I took it personally. A city's creativity doesn't fuel itself, you know.

And quite often, it felt like the whole city spilled into the café, clanging and jostling. Corrine and I worked with over-caffeinated intensity as food and people steadily heated up. Somehow, the owner knew to appear from his room upstairs just before we cracked. In a stoned haze, he would turn back the tempo of the background beats. Ahhh, Nick Drake. Pink Moon was the soundtrack of relief that summer.

That Sunday, people were up and down Acland Street like usual. Our morning regulars had come and gone, and we were readying ourselves for the lunch rush. Corrine stopped mid-way through making a latte, put the half-warm milk down, and went to the window. Wooden, she stared out at the street. In the absence of her usual breezy commentary I joined her at the window and asked what she was doing. "She looks suspicious," she replied, pointing to a woman – dressed in black, of course. The woman was walking up the street with her daughter. "She could be a terrorist," Corrine added seriously, tracking her until she was out of view.

Acland Street was a street like all streets. It was a street through which some bodies would move, either unnoticed or as noticeably charming or quirky; inviting commentary from behind the bread baskets. And it was a street through which other bodies would move, only to be inspected, feared, and hated.

I didn't say anything to Corrine that day, though my stomach gripped tight with her words. Wanting to be part of the white-shiny world she'd helped open up, I thought confrontation might have expelled me from it. I was still coming to terms with what those burning towers would mean now for people who looked like that woman. And for people who looked like me.

In the days and months and years to follow, those terms would become clear.

I wouldn't be so quiet, now, looking out on Acland with Corrine.

Chapel Street
by ALYSSA COOMBS

A TWILIGHT DREAM

Acland Street, St Kilda

OLIVIA SHENKEN

The Acland Street of my childhood is a kingdom of summer. I've known it in winter too, but in my memory it is a kind of talisman, a lodestone, the longest day of the year. That same Acland Street is also an endless evening, falling into dusk.

It's like one of those planets that always have the same side facing their sun, and the other turned out to space in eternal night. The narrow boundary between them might be liveable. Stand close enough to the sunlit side to feel the edge of the beating heat. Look out towards the darkness, maybe on a hilltop with a sombre view. Forever blanketed in starlight – that's Acland Street.

Wrapped in a towel with my Mr. Whippy ice cream, I'd watch the sunset from the promenade – red and shimmering, blinding on the water.

I'd always try, with a childlike idiosyncrasy, to get from the water to the promenade without getting my feet sandy again. After I failed, I'd just enjoy the sensation of the sand, not the softest in the world, but still sand with its give and take. I'd get to the taps to wash off all the grains, and try and fail again to get it all off. I'd walk around barefoot until the sand rubbed off onto the concrete, but still there'd be some sticking to my calf. Some would always get under my fingernails too, and when I blinked I knew there must be some in the corner-crinkles of my eyes. The salt of the bay would follow me with the sand.

My brother would have been down at the skate park, wheeling and gliding, flying with a grace I'd never have. But the rest of us, my parents and sisters, would walk down to meet a family friend. He owned a café or bar, I'm not sure which. And it doesn't really matter so much, because in the Acland Street of my memory the only drink is hot chocolate. Always served with marshmallows. I've lost my taste for it now, but chocolatey milk and sugary fluff is mixed in with the flour and water of me, mingled with salt and sand and the odour of rubbish and the warmth of a car seat after a swim.

Rubbish. Yes. Noises and smells I didn't understand, men and women on the street whose eyes I avoided even then. Broken glass, litter on the sand. Summer doesn't mean clean.

But I was with my parents, and safe and warm and dried by my towel. I still had sand on my legs, and in my hair.

That friend of my parents, who owned that shadowy half-forgotten place, had a dog. Pogo. A neurotic, aging, possessive Jack Russell. We babysat him often, until his owner moved to Tasmania. He took to my eldest sister, and would snarl and snap when she tried to move him from her lap. Still, I wanted him with me. After Pogo left our life, we adopted a Cairn Terrier. He stretches on from that era to now, his puppyhood long past. But, in the Acland Street of those years, we only had a Part-Time Terrier, and I petted him as I drank my hot chocolate.

If the ice cream wasn't Mr Whippy, it was 7Apples. My siblings would get the apple pie flavour. I never really knew what to ask for. I'd default to something simple like chocolate, then beg the others for a try of theirs. Unsurprisingly, I'm a youngest child.

Walking back to the car from Acland Street always scared me a little. By then it would be night, not just dusk. But I walked behind my dad and felt safe there.

Now that I think about it, a shiver comes into the mix. Maybe it wasn't always summer there. Not even summer is summer in this city. Yes, a definite shiver, mixed in with the scent of salt, the feel of sand rubbing off damp skin. The hot chocolate tasted even better for the sharp breeze, for the remnants of salt I licked off my lips. A spring beach day, maybe, or the last gasp of autumn.

Was it just one day? Can't be. One archetypal day, maybe, coalesced, averaged from all of them. Days, spread across years, spread across a mug of hot chocolate.

I'm not a coffee person, but hold a hot cup of anything in your hands and tell me you don't feel something. If I hold a cup of tea, let the ceramic warm up, let my skin warm from it – then I hear the seagulls on St Kilda beach, the sea breeze, screams from Luna Park. Despite my fear of rollercoasters, on every walk from the beach to Acland Street through the carpark I'd look up, see the whitewashed wooden slats of the Scenic Railway, and wish I was up there screaming with them.

Wish I was on that ride, wish I ordered the apple pie ice cream, wish I had a dog. Wishful thinking. Now I have to keep from wishing myself Back Then. I don't really want to be seven years old again. No way.

But it'd be nice to watch a St Kilda sunset on a summer day. Not alone, as I've done recently, but with my family again, whoever they may be. Though it might not feel the same if instead of hot chocolate I'm cradling a tea, or a chai latte, or something else in my palms, and if I'm not seven but rather seven-times-three.

And if we walked back up to Acland Street, through the carpark again, looking up at the roller-coaster – the Scenic Railway is out of order again – it would be different. Unsurprisingly, a decade and more has brought change. It isn't really the same place to me. Now I can wander through the Twilight Market and recognise the smell of weed. I know that the homeless men and women and the drunks aren't just bogeymen wandering out of the night to scare children. I know that the water is cleaner in other parts of the bay. I don't party with the backpackers on New Year's. Is it because they would have scared seven-year-old me?

Last summer, I took a trip with my dad to the beach in the afternoon. There had been a cool change, and no one else was there. Cold, wind, sand. We gave up after a few minutes.

Now I have different reasons to go down to Acland Street. Readings, mostly. I work at another bookshop in a different part of the city, but that one is my favourite, my happy place. I once met someone there, and we spoke about books, and we never met again. I could spend hours browsing, picking a book off the shelf, staring entranced at intricate cover-art, failing to repress the habitual urge to straighten and re-shelve books as I go.

But also window-shopping. Acland Street must echo with my longing thoughts as I stare at sleek mannequins and feel the silken texture of dresses between my fingers. I imagine myself wearing one of those dresses, surrounded by friends I love, back out on the beach eating fish and chips, or boisterous in one of those restaurants or bars that play music so loud you can hear it from the other side of the street, with crowds that spill out onto the pavement. When I was young, I'd have had to walk in my dad's wake just to get through. But in my imagination it's just me and my friends, drunk, loud, warm in the dusk.

It's strangely comforting to watch the 96 tram begin and end its journey there on Acland. The pedestrians casually crossing the road don't speed up at all as the tram chimes its warning and rattles slowly down the street. At one point I had to tram to Fitzroy Street in the evenings to get to work. A nice, scenic route: Acland Street, Luna Park, the Esplanade. I'd look out the window to see it, not just to avoid eye contact with the people sitting near me.

One of my other favourite places is the community garden. Its location is perfect: corner Shakespeare Grove and Chaucer Street. It makes me want to cry, going there. That place, that little Eden, also only exists for me in summer. I'm afraid winter would break the perfect illusion, though it's always possible it might just enhance it. I won't describe it for you. Go see it for yourself. Maybe it's just me.

Have you ever been to Acland Cakes? Monarch? Europa? I had a kugelhopf from Monarch today. My dad can't set foot on Acland Street without extolling the deliciousness of that kugelhopf. He's still around, and so are the cake shops. But they won't be forever. Acland Street, the real Acland Street, is not a solid thing. It is ephemeral, partly a memory of 2005, partly my reflections on it today. Kugelhopf or marshmallows? Sand and damp skin, or paging through a paperback and falling in futile love?

If I wrote a play, I might give the setting as Acland Street. And if that play were produced, someone would decide on the props, the set. The sunset, maybe the clown-face of Luna Park there in the background. A neon "7Apples" sign, a tram, the chalkboard outside Readings with a new quote at the start of each new scene. I don't even know what Acland Street is to me. A fairyland of my earlier years, not only the happy sprites but the dark fairies too. Shakespeare Grove with its enchanted garden is only a little way away. Revelry, fear, light – indistinct shadows of a midsummer night.

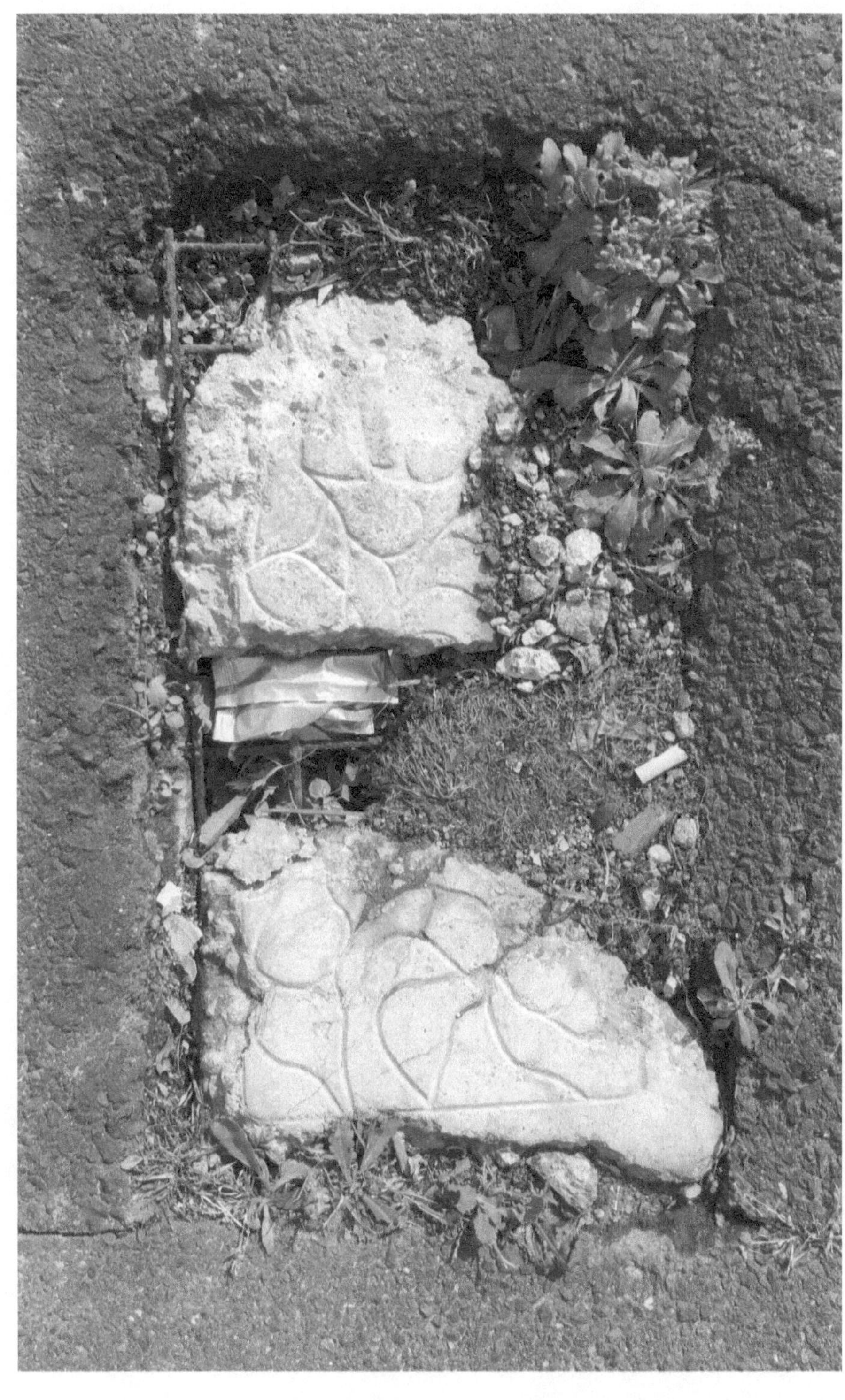

SPOUT

Glen Eira Road, Ripponlea

ALLAN LAKE

At this Ripponlea cafe
music is way too rocky
for my mellow taste. Tables
too close together – *excuse
me, love*, he apologises after
touching a stranger, while
trying to settle. But the place,
commonplace as name suggests,
is crowded with devotees, not
of teapots but of rugelach
with its debatable spelling,
its now utterly decorative ch.

There's rugelach and there's
rugelach as no saying goes.
Nor do people on Glen Eira Road
say: *Don't google; be sticky*,
but someone should.

These homely delights are hand-
crafted by an ancient handmaiden
according to bearded barista,
who is in a position to know.
(upright at coffee machine)
May she live forever whether she
wants to or not, I say. Just one
rugelach can counteract every bitter
article in a newspaper and you can
peruse entire paper while nibbling
and sipping your shot of espresso.

People and time sit quite still
in the rugezone because some-
where deep then deeper within,
they are savouring a small,
sweet moment with
themselves.

West

A FLUTTER ON THE MONKEYS

NICK GADD

"Ever heard of White City?" asked the writer and historian Tony Birch, as we sat in his office at Melbourne Uni. "Greyhound track out Sunshine way, gone now. It used to be very popular." Tony pulled up a website called "Melbourne 1945", which shows aerial photos of the greater urban area of Melbourne in 1945, and allows you to compare the city then with aerial views of the same places today. We squinted at the screen together as he scrolled over black-and-white images of the western suburbs, zooming in on Sunshine Road, which begins just south of the footy oval in West Footscray and heads west alongside the railway line towards Sunshine via Tottenham. Back then there were not many houses out that way, and few factories. Just the road, a railway line and paddocks. A couple of quarries. A single tiny platform in the middle of nowhere. And south of that, a faint white oval etched into the earth. "*That's* the dog track," Tony said triumphantly.

...

I've been exploring the Melbourne suburbs for several years now, and I'm drawn to vanished places and secret histories. The lost dog track grabbed my attention for these reasons rather than any interest in racing or gambling. It's undeniably true, though, that sporting activities are one of the royal roads to understanding Melbourne.

So one day in August, Lynne and I set out on foot on a quest for White City. We started out at the Whitten Oval, back in 1945 the home of Footscray Football Club, now (after narrowly escaping merger by extinction) the Western Bulldogs. The statue of Ted Whitten stands out the front, sending a booming kick over the oval named in his honour. Were we proudly wearing our Bulldogs caps, that day? I don't know, but let's say we were. On Grand Final day 2016 we had been here, watching the glorious victory on the big screen, surrounded by fellow Bulldog fans. The team could do no wrong that miraculous day, and as the red-white-and-blue stormed home in the final quarter, and the excitement raged around us, we'd felt connected to the spirit of the place.

We walked from West Footscray along Sunshine Road, the *whoomp-whoomp* of cars passing us, drivers giving odd glances at the strange sight of a couple on foot, our eyes and ears alert for clues about the past. Despite its name, there is nothing pretty about Sunshine Road. These days it's a place of factories (mostly closed), For Lease signs, bus depots, smash repairers and container yards. But it's a good place for industrial archeology. James Flood, the maker and restorer of vintage cars, once had its premises here, and its painted signage still adorns the walls; so did Imperial Chemicals, and Goldsbrough Mort, the mighty agribusiness whose wool stores used to be a commanding presence throughout Australia. Today the wool store has been converted into a storage place: we may not manufacture stuff in Melbourne these days, but we certainly store it. The former Uncle Tobys factory is still here, maker of a billion breakfasts, but it's now occupied by someone else, though there's a sign that says "CREAMOTA" lurking on one of the chimneys, like the ghost of porridge past.

We reached the big new Tottenham station, and the odd little collection of shops that huddles in the shadow of the overpass: a tattoo place, a hairdresser, an "antique" shop selling secondhand electric scooters, nude mannequins and a skeleton, perhaps a refugee from some medical department. Above the shops, on one of the pediments, Lynne spotted a sign reading "Hansen for Houses", dated 1947. Hansen was a prolific builder of houses in these suburbs, and a key figure in their post-war development: many locals are living in Hansen's houses to this day.

When we reached the site between Olympia Street and Quarry Road we found not a dog track, but the Olex cable-making factory. There's a plaque on the wall recording that the factory was opened by Prime Minister the Rt Hon. Robert Menzies CH QC MP on 4 April 1960. That was the era when the suburban fringe was opened up for industrial development, a time of economic optimism: people living in Hansen's houses would have come here (and Imperial Chemicals, Goldsbrough Mort, Uncle Tobys) to find work. But the factory was on the verge of closure that day. I don't know what we thought we might find as we wandered around the perimeter, picking our way between piles of trash – abandoned mattresses, pallets, all the usual crap you find in suburban edge-lands – and peeking through fences, but all evidence of the dog track had long gone.

Today, if you want to know about White City, you can research a few facts via old newspapers and history societies, but it can only be revisited in the imagination.

...

The name originated in London, where greyhound racing with mechanical hares rather than live ones (as in the bloody sport of coursing) was all the rage. Copycat White Cities sprang up in Manchester, Glasgow, Cardiff, even Tasmania. The new technology was already in use at Sydney's Glebe Circuit, where it attracted huge crowds. In the west of Melbourne, a group of entrepreneurs saw an opportunity to provide cheap entertainment. In

1927 the Victorian Mechanical Hare Association set up a greyhound racing stadium on a patch of empty land on Sunshine Road, mid-way between Tottenham and Sunshine stations.

There wasn't so much activity along Sunshine Road in those days, but quarries were close by and it wasn't far to the abattoirs and factories of Footscray and Sunshine. Greyhound racing has always been a working-class sport. While equine thoroughbreds change hands for millions, an ordinary person gains just as much pleasure from training or watching a racing dog at a fraction of the cost. Besides that, you can bet small sums at the dog track, and you don't have to get dressed up. It looked like the shareholders in White City had backed a winner: the first meeting attracted 8,000 punters, along with 40 bookmakers. The shareholders were elated. What could possibly go wrong?

Unexpectedly, White City was the target of political intervention. The state government claimed that betting on greyhounds was a pursuit from which the lower classes must be protected. Acting with astonishing speed, the Attorney General, Mr Slater, introduced a bill on 6 December 1927 to ban mechanical coursing. During debate, Sir William McPherson MP complained that "the greater portion of the persons who attend these meetings are boys and girls who are able to make bets as low as two shillings. Surely we do not want to encourage such a class of entertainment." Mr McKenzie MP referred to "degrading and revolting scenes" and claimed that "anyone who does not support a Bill of this kind is not standing up for the morals of the community".

The aspect that most greatly alarmed the gentlemen of the house was that women seemed to like it. Said Mr Gray MP, "Only a few days ago I had a conversation with a friend . . . He is a great sporting man, and he took the opportunity while in London to attend a tin-hare coursing meeting. He told me there was a crowd there of 72,000 people. There were 500 bookmakers. The din was something awful . . .

The vast majority of the people present were women. Many women had young children trailing at their skirts, and some had babies at their breasts. He watched these women put their one or two shillings on the dogs. He told me that he thought it was a dreadful thing."[1]

But what did the honourable gentlemen really have against the working people's sport? In truth, the legislation was all about defending the interests of the horse racing fraternity. Mr Toutcher, member for Stawell and Ararat, pointed out that "there is a very strong and monopolistic [horse] racing man in this community, who . . . has influence which he has exercised to a very alarming and considerable degree." His words were unheeded, and the bill duly passed. Tin-hare greyhound racing was banned because it might lure gamblers away from horse racing.

Without mechanical hares White City had lost its biggest attraction, and the passing of the Bill bankrupted the shareholders. That was when a white knight, Fred Watkins, stepped in. Fred was an entrepreneur with a bit of PT Barnum about him, and he dreamed up a range of novelties to entice the punters back. He brought in live hares instead of tin hares, and held not just greyhound races but whippet races, goat races, professional foot races, and most exotically of all, greyhounds with monkey jockeys.

I had my doubts the first time I heard about this. Monkey jockeys sounded like an urban legend, far too silly and cruel to be true. But true it is: monkey jockeys were a thing. Capuchin monkeys can be trained to cling to the sinuous backs of greyhounds as they reach speeds of 70 kph. Even in 1938 that was seen as a bit outrageous: the Victorian Society for the Protection of Animals condemned the use of monkeys as cruel (no one seems to have been too concerned about the welfare of

1. The Parliamentary quotes are taken from Hansard, Legislative Assembly, 6 December 1927, p3148.

the dogs). But the stunt did its job in generating publicity. *The Argus*, one of Melbourne's major newspapers, gave two monkeys named "Pike" and "Badger" a run on Page 3 on 11 May 1938, along with photographs that remove all doubt.

Tottenham White City was a red-hot attraction from the 1930s to the 1950s. There were three meetings a week, with total weekly attendances around 9,000. During the Depression, thousands of working-class families reared and raced greyhounds, so the dogs kept many a household up and running. (Where the monkeys came from, I don't know.) White City had its own station, serviced on race days by the Dog Train. It must have been quite something to catch the Dog Train to White City for a flutter on the monkeys.

Eventually the crowds declined, and after 28 years the venue closed, on 29 December 1955. In a final irony, on the first day of 1956 the *Dog Races Act* came into force, which lifted the ban on mechanical coursing and banned racing with live hares, reversing the legislation of 1927. Fred Watkins sold the track and equipment for 113,000 pounds. A couple of years later, the cable factory was there. Now that too is closed, and the site awaits its next incarnation.

White City, a place of raucous energy and community life, is silenced as if it had never existed. It's preserved only in a few news clippings and photographs, and the faint memories of old-timers. The station hung on for a while, used by Olex workers, until it closed in the 1980s. There are no ruins, no signs, and no official history.

But maybe on a quiet night on Sunshine Road if you listen hard enough, you might just catch the echo of a distant crowd cheering on the greyhounds and their monkey jockeys.

THE REAL STATE OF RAY'S REAL ESTATE

Berry Street, Yarraville

MICHELLE FINCKE

'Tis the season for real estate hyperbole, and the sales board for the scrubbed and renovated little weatherboard across the road – featuring an elegant living-room with gleaming floorboards – declares it "the best it's ever been".

But before the stainless-steel appliances and the stunning, fully-tiled bathroom, the house belonged to Ray. Ray and Nelly. Nelly was Ray's dog, a warm-hearted shaggy mongrel with a perpetual grin, fleas and a prodigious stink. Sometimes, Ray would head up the bush to shoot with a mate and Nelly would swim in the cool river, before rolling in manure and rotting corpses for the long drive home.

She may not have been particularly smart, but she was wonderfully optimistic and devoted to Ray. There were imaginary possums in their gnarly nature-strip tree, and at his urging – "Get the possums, Nelly!" – she'd leap high, nipping at their invisible tails to the delight of the kids growing up in Berry Street.

Ray adored Nelly. He used a bit of old rope for a lead and she was never registered. His neighbours formed an anxious coalition guarding against the ranger, gently recommending flea treatments and immunisations to no avail. Ray himself tenderly cared for other people's dogs, popping them into safety in his backyard with a huge, straggly lemon tree and a bird in a cage, until he could gleefully reunite owner and stray.

When we moved into Ray's neighbourhood in inner-west Yarraville, part of the predictable diaspora seeking affordable real estate, community and a place to start a family, he was in his early eighties and had lived in Berry Street, in various dwellings, for much of his life. One day, he ambled across the road to show me a treasure, a crumpled black and white photo he'd found of my house, taken in the 1950s; it was a fresh-faced stranger, peeking out from under a coquettish hedge. If he bore a grudge about the arrival of SUVs, state-of-the-art prams and architect-imagined extensions – the gentrification of his historic, working-class suburb – he never let on.

His final home in Berry Street was on the corner opposite our place, but really, he lived on the nature strip. Clad in year-round uniform of shorts and baggy blue singlet, it was where he stood vigilant, sensitive to the thrum of daily life and determined not to let it pass by without his notice. He bent the ears of tradies, exchanged g'days with schoolkids on scooters and watched us all come and go, a surging domestic tide: strapping toddlers into car seats, hauling in armfuls of groceries, racing off to work. "Geez, you've been busy, Love!" he'd marvel, the only person through the long day to notice.

He'd walk Nelly and, now and then, drive his ute wonkily to the shops for a bag full of austere essentials. He loved to spend brisk winter afternoons watching the local footy, as he had for decades, and afterwards settle in for a few beers at the club. An ex-serviceman, he'd go to the RSL and, somewhat grumpily, by taxi to the doctor who, invariably, had *no idea* and would prescribe pills that *never* made him feel better and *obviously* weren't worth taking. So he didn't.

On sunny afternoons he'd limp across the road to lean on the picket fence and admire our cat, who'd strike various adorable poses for his benefit. "Handsome cat, that" he'd exclaim gruffly. He'd put on silly voices and make the kids squeal with laughter.

Ray declined all but a couple of invitations for a cuppa; when cornered, he perched awkwardly, a Stubbies-clad buttock hanging off the chair ready for a quick escape. We'd struggle through the pleasantries until we got to the somewhat safer turf of the life of Berry Street, where workers' cottages mingled with red-brick Edwardians, smart homes for the industrial gentry. He'd gulp his hot, milky tea and, after a little strained conversation, bolt for the front fence, happy to yarn for hours on neutral territory.

Neighbourly kindness had to be repaid. *Had to be.* Mow his nature strip, long-neck bottles of beer would appear on your mat. Give him mince pies on a paper plate or a container of leftover Christmas turkey, he'd fire back with an armful of chocolate Santas for the kids. A jar of jam equalled a fistful of Tatts tickets. Hearing that our little boy loved aeroplanes, Ray shyly gifted him an old book about military aircraft. I tried to thank him, but he was already sprinting home, singlet fluttering in the breeze.

Once, I took him a meal. He reluctantly invited me to bring the plate of Gladwrapped lasagne into his careworn, gloomy kitchen and we both stood, awkward and silent, staring at the floor. Trespassing, I felt I had trodden on his shadow.

Pain from various ailments caused insomnia and he prowled the darkened Berry Street like a battle-scarred tom cat, foiling robberies. No Neighbourhood Watch could ever out-watch Ray. He bellowed and fiercely brandished his walking stick at thieves trying to lift Navmans from dashboards and builders' tools from vans, earning himself local superhero status.

He was a widower, cared for by three feisty female neighbours. Ray drove them crazy: "won't take his medicine . . . doesn't eat properly . . . never listens." They exasperated him with their constant interfering! I saw a cold stand-off in the no-man's-land middle of Berry Street over a brown paper-wrapped parcel tied tightly with string. Inside, apparently, was a striped pair of men's flannelette pyjamas that Esme had bought from the legendary department store Forges of Footscray. She was certain – *certain* – he needed them. He *definitely* did not, and they both fumed for days.

When one of Ray's informal carers, his near-neighbour Glenys, succumbed to cancer at home, he stood a sombre vigil on his patch of turf, barrel-chest balanced on spindly legs, dignified grief laid bare.

The years passed and his steps became less sure, the taxi rides to the useless doctor more frequent, the ute purely decorative. He was still good for a chat, but his memory was hazier and the manual mower with which he doggedly tackled the pocket-handkerchief nature strip now quietly rusted in the shed.

Early one morning the ambulance came and took Ray to hospital after the last of many falls, and as we sadly watched him being driven away, we knew he would never return. He wouldn't see our children become teenagers and, with the L-plates crooked on windscreens, take their first tentative lurches down Berry Street.

He wouldn't see the decommissioned trade school turned into boutique townhouses, nor Esme finally swamped by the dementia she fought like a tigress with long bracing walks and weekly aqua aerobics. He wouldn't see the next bloom of babies in Berry Street: the new SUVs, the next-generation prams, the harried new parents nipping into each other's houses for a quick glass of wine and a chat.

He wouldn't stand in the middle of Berry Street on New Year's Eve to watch the fireworks illuminate the city on the other the side of the

Maribyrnong, a city now bristling with cranes and apartment towers and, most unexpectedly, a Ferris wheel with disco lighting. And he wouldn't see Nelly's possum tree, a twisted ornamental plum livid with pink frills in spring, collapse with the sheer weight of the years not long after he had gone. The council replaced it with a silvery olive, the one tree sure to outlive us all.

After the ambulance carrying Ray wheeled out of Berry Street, life stalked mercilessly on; Nelly was adopted by kind-hearted locals, registered, walked on a leash and washed frequently.

Ray didn't last long in the nursing home. No one thought he would.

At the funeral we, his neighbours, stood among a chapel full of strangers and realised we barely knew Ray. In his little house across from us in Berry Street, there were whole rooms unseen, hints of dark corners. All these years we'd just been peering through the dusty windows, catching glimpses. Which was fair enough.

But still we mourned our loss and wept for Ray: animal-lover, returned serviceman, footy fan, fearless neighbourhood watcher and the generous soul of Berry Street. His house was sold and filled with young tenants, thumping music and pizza boxes. Then they too were gone, and an army of tradies laboured all through the dreary winter.

It's a nice little house. Every element conveys contemporary quality behind a classical image. That's what the board says, but I still can't bring myself to inspect Ray's house, to tread on his shadow.

I know real estate speak is necessarily extravagant and that houses, like men, in their time play many parts. But the best it's ever been? It's not even close.

FROM KORUMBURRA TO KINGSVILLE

HELEN CERNE

Highway by highway, the remorseless cars
Strangle the city, put it out of pain.
Melbourne, Chris Wallace-Crabbe

...

"I don't like West Footscray. It's ugly, it's noisy and it pongs. There are only factories, shops and houses. And Somerville Road's too busy to play on."

"What about the smell of the butter factory in Korumburra?" asks Mum.

There should be something special about leaving Gippsland and shifting to live in the city of Melbourne in 1956, when the Olympic Games will soon be on, but it doesn't feel that way.

"I'm not going to that big, red brick double-storey school," I shout at Mum, storming off, a stubborn eight-year-old girl missing her horse and pet goat. I'm determined to be miserable.

Across the smoke-stained sky of a winter afternoon, I hear car horns, sirens, beeps, but also the drone hum of industry across the western suburbs. There is no sound like it. Everything in this suburb is bigger, busier and different. Korumburra seems so far away.

We live in an old weatherboard next to a service station, opposite a greengrocer's and a butcher's in Somerville Road, West Footscray (named Kingsville in this local area) which is choking with fumes and traffic. An old chook pen in the backyard is my new playhouse, and when I stare out through the wire at this ugly, bare garden with its patch of dying lawn and one geranium plant, I feel trapped. Where are ferns, flowers, and birds that sweep and dart, chirp and sing?

This road is too busy for cricket or chasey. Dad says the suburb is expanding quickly as there's the constant arrival of New Australians looking for jobs and homes creating extra traffic. A migrant hostel in Millers Road, Brooklyn, houses some of the influx of residents. The many factories and the large abattoirs of Smorgons, Borthwicks and Gilbertsons make the awful smells and smoky skies but offer work for these new arrivals. I screw up my nose at the stink of dead meat constantly in the Footscray air.

"I hate this house and I'm not going to that school."

"Come on, I'll walk with you. It won't be too bad. You'll make a friend." My warm mother is trying to defrost me. "Your father needed this change of a job. Your brother likes his new high school. Now, now Miss Sulky Puss, we're all together and that's what really counts." How does she only have the ability to make me feel bad by encouraging me to be good?

We walk up our new street past the shops to school. The greengrocer is Mr Moretti – a dark man who can't speak much English. Every morning, he carefully polishes and arranges his fruit, particularly apples, the Jonathans and Granny Smiths, in crisp clean rows; spreads out banana hands in curved layers, rearranges firm navels and Valencias with their bright orange faces next to black-purple grapes all frosty-looking. From the ceiling hang coloured streamers, and around the walls the local Boon Spa soft drink bottles of every flavour: raspberry, cola, ginger beer, lemony squash, orange, lime, my favourite, creamy soda, and my worst choice, black sarsaparilla.

"Oranges and lemons, oranges and lemons say the bells of St Clemens." I start chanting the rhyme sang at kids' parties. "Chop, chop, chop the last man's head off, off, off, off, off!" That's how I feel walking along this truck-filled road to my new school.

Next door to the fruiterer is the fish and chip shop run by a Greek called Nick. On his walls there's picture ads of Coke and Chiko rolls. Above a pinball machine in the corner are rude photos, one of a young woman with a pony tail bending over in a low cut blouse, and another of a pretty blonde lying across a long smooth limousine showing her pants. Already my older brother has had free chips from Nick and reckons you learn a lot after two days in the city. Mum and I pass a delicatessen with strange-shaped cheeses and red sausages hanging above the counter. A strong smell of fried onions is in the air and it is only quarter-to-nine in the morning.

At Kingsville Primary, No. 3988, a large red brick building waiting for victims, I am put in grade three. I miss my backyard, my animals, my cubby, my Gippsland green rolling hills and my old friends. I'm lonely, determined to be unhappy in this school full of hundreds of city kids. No-one talks to me at first. I sit anxious, afraid of failure, scared of being alone in the noisy playground.

At morning play, the enormous yard is full of shouting children running and catching balls, playing skippy and hidey. I stand apart still with the fear of loneliness creeping up inside. Suddenly, a girl from my grade comes up to me with a warm grin. She has big hazel eyes, a sweet smile, brown hair in long plaits looped by ribbons, and takes me by hand to the mothers' club stall where she gives me threepence for a toffee. It's sticky, sweet and delicious. I lick the hundreds and thousands stuck on top.

"I'm Lisbete from Latvia."

"I'm Helen from Korumburra."

She shows me around the ground and then we play a game called Sevens, which consists of throwing and catching a ball in a variety of ways against the brick school wall. At the end of a long first day Lisbete walks me home along Somerville Road showing me the best milk bar for lollies. You can buy a mixed bag for just sixpence! Or a handful of raspberries, bullets or jujubes for even less. Another shop sells ice-creams that are dipped in warm, yummy chocolate that sets hard. They are dear, but something to look forward to. Lisbete lives just around the corner from our house. What luck!

"How was your first day?" Mum asks, handing me a cup of Milo. I frown then make a sad face. I'm not happy, but it could be worse.

The next Saturday, Lisbete and I walk to the Sun picture theatre in Yarraville for the afternoon flicks. I can't believe there are two cinemas in walking distance and four more in Footscray, only a bus or tram ride away. The Sun and St George are situated on either side of the Yarraville railway station, less than a mile from where we live. It's a long walk, yet I don't even notice, happy to be with a new friend. I am also keen to see how city kids behave by themselves at the arvo matinee. It's the first time Mum has let me go to the pictures on my own.

Yarraville is an older Melbourne suburb with tiny streets and cramped, ageing shops, some selling remnants and oddments. One big department store on a corner is called Fred's, and Lisbete reckons they sell everything there. She loves going to the pictures even though the films are more for boys – about pirates, soldiers and cowboys. After the newsreel, there is a serial with what my brother calls "a vile villain" chasing a distressed maiden along a railway track. The train gets her, and all the kids are booing and stamping their feet. My heart is pounding as the beautiful star goes under the wheels.

"Don't worry," shouts Lisbete, licking her black Choo-choo bar, "she'll be okay next week. You'll see."

The following Saturday we smuggle in greasy potato fritters covered in salt and vinegar in our red vinyl bucket-bags. At interval there is live entertainment, with a clown or local tap dancers or even a magician to keep the kids entertained. Lucky dips, and Lisbete says sometimes prizes of small kewpie dolls are given away. This is fabulous fun; much better than the Korumburra matinees. Whenever there is too much talking in the film the kids just chat, but as soon as there's a chase or a fight or kissing, the theatre comes alive with whistles, shouts, applause or stamping feet.

"You city kids got no manners," I say to my new pal.

She ignores me, too wrapped up in the story on the big screen. I get my Dixie ice-cream all over my new fuzzy-wuzzy pink bolero and my fingers become greasy from the chips. As we walk home along the busy suburban street, we become the film stars of the future.

Lisbete's house is a small, neat, white weatherboard with a well-kept garden. Inside there are pretty ornaments and coloured paintings, one of angelic children surrounded by flowers and animals in pastel colours. Her mother is a friendly woman who gushes with a strong accent when she speaks and makes me feel very welcome. I do not meet Lisbete's father as he's asleep after long shift work in the ICI chemical plant in Yarraville. Out the back of her house is a little bungalow with another migrant couple living in it. Her parents lived there when they first came to the suburb, while their weatherboard was being built. Behind her place is a polluted creek that runs through miles of thistle paddocks, where newly made roads etch their way through the barren wilderness to make a new housing estate. Stoney Creek is murky grey and oily and even more smelly than the air.

Within a fortnight my family settle in to Somerville Road, West Footscray. My brother and I can't run wild and play as we did in Gippsland, but we have found other things to do. At the intersection of our street with Williamstown Road we can catch a tram into bigger and even busier Footscray, which has more shops, more cinemas, even bigger department and furniture stores. My mother buys us new clothes and shoes but only goes window-shopping for herself. At the other end of Somerville Road there's a large, busy intersection where Geelong Road and Roberts Street converge, and a big café called Sam's Coffee Pot where truck drivers stop. My brother's only twelve but he has been there with his mates, bought a greasy hamburger and played the juke box. They have rock 'n' roll hits like Elvis Presley's "Hound Dog" and Bill Haley's "See You Later, Alligator". My brother reckons it's like being a real American teenager!

In late November the world comes to our city with the Olympic Games. Television arrives at the same time, so we now can watch exciting things on the small screens in the windows of bigger retailers. TV changes everything – the way we spend our time, the way we see others, and the way we see ourselves.

One evening just after tea, Dad drives us around the corner, down Williamstown Road to the Massey car showrooms to watch an AMV TV in the window. A large crowd are already there on the Yarraville footpath, watching the events on the black-and-white screen. Two ladies have brought foldup chairs, a few little kids already in their pyjamas have rugs and cushions, but most families prefer to stand. A large boy steps on my toes but I refuse to move away, too absorbed by the Australians Lorraine Crapp and Dawn Fraser swimming for gold to even notice him elbowing in. Even the advertisements for Pelaco shirts or Tarax soft drinks we watch in awe.

Suddenly it's goodbye to the wireless – to *Hop Harrigan, Larry Kent, Private Eye, Life with Dexter, Caltex Theatre, Jack Davey, Pick a Box, The Argonauts*. My big brother and I watch with envy as antennas start appearing across the neighbourhood, some along Somerville Road. My parents say TVs are far too expensive and we will have to be patient. Most mums don't work and rely on the male wage, so most children switch tack and nag their dads to get this magic box full of action and stories. Lisbete now wants to be a TV star.

"Annie Oakley's on after tea, Mum. Please can I go to Mrs Brown's?" I beg my mother after school. "All the kids will be talking about it tomorrow."

"I thought we were going to play cards." Mum looks disappointed. Our close-knit family is growing apart, changing quickly in the city.

"We can play that anytime. Besides *Rin Tin Tin* is on after. He's the best dog in the whole world!"

Television alters family life. Cinemas start to lose business. Dad says the Sun and St George in Yarraville may have to close. Reading and homework are done quickly because whenever we can, my brother and I run to the few Kingsville houses with TV. Sometimes we take hot chips from Nick's to share, sometimes we take a special bag of mixed lollies, sometimes we take a new mate to squash up on the neighbour's sofa with all the other kids. Sometimes the host makes toast for supper.

"I like living here," I finally tell my parents one night after tea on my way out to watch the latest Davy Crocket episode just up the street.

"What about the smells, the noise and the traffic?" asks Mum.

"What smell? We live in a big city, what do you expect?"

ABOUT THE CONTRIBUTORS

Anna Kate Blair is a writer from Aotearoa. She has previously had work published in journals and books including *The Appendix*, *Litro*, *King's Review*, *The Island Review* and *10 Stories: Writing About Architecture*. She holds a PhD from the University of Cambridge.

Helen Cerne is a poet and novelist. Her works include the poetry collection *Just Heart Work* and the novels *Those Who Can't*, *Circling Lina* and *Shifting*, written with her late partner, Serge. Helen taught creative writing at Victoria University for many years.

Rijn Collins is an award-winning Melbourne writer, with over 100 short stories published in anthologies and journals, performed at literary festivals, and broadcast on ABC Radio National. In 2016 she placed first in the Sarah Awards for International Audio Fiction in New York. Her debut novel will be published by Scribner. www.rijncollins.com.

Alyssa Coombs is a graphic designer and illustrator who has spent most of her adult life living and working in Melbourne. She designed this book, and is a humble inner city coffee snob. www.alyssacoombs.com.au

Johanna Ellersdorfer has lived in eight different cities over the past ten years, including two stints in Melbourne. She is currently based in Sydney, where she writes, paints and restores art.

Michelle Fincke's writing life began as a cadet journalist at *The Herald* in Melbourne, and she's worked with words – at newspapers, magazines and as a writing teacher – ever since. She has deep ties to the West, loves travelling with her family and has an inexplicable passion for the Tour de France.

Sarah Fraser is a medical writer who moonlights as an author and publisher. She is the author of three books for younger readers: *Dinosaur Danger!*, *Where's my Mummy?* and *The Secret of the Catacombs*. Her work has been published in *The Age*, *lip* magazine and *Hide and Seek: Melbourne*. www.quietcorner.com.au.

Nick Gadd is the author of two novels: *Ghostlines*, set in Yarraville, which won a Victorian Premier's Literary Award and a Ned Kelly Award, and his latest book, *Death of a Typographer*. He is the author of the blog Melbourne Circle, which describes a journey on foot circling the whole of Melbourne, beginning in Williamstown.

Sheila Graham is a former Brunswick resident. Now an art student and occasional stand-up comedian, she is a current resident of Glasgow, and still misses solo boozing on Lygon Street.

Bea Jones has been submitting her poetry to anthologies and doing live readings since the early 1990s. She moved to Melbourne from Newcastle in 1998, and loves this vibrant, diverse city. Bea was shortlisted for the Grieve Writing Competition (poetry) and the ACU Prize for Poetry in 2019, and in 2016 won the Ada Cambridge Poetry Prize.

Originally from Saskatchewan, **Allan Lake** has lived in Vancouver, Cape Breton Island, Ibiza, Tasmania and, for now, Melbourne. He has two collections published: Tasmanian Tiger Breaks Silence (1988) and Sand in the Sole (2014). Allan won the Elwood (Aus) Poetry Prize (2016), Lost Tower Publications (UK) Poetry Comp (2017) and the Dan Poets competition at the Melbourne Spoken Word and Poetry Festival in 2018.

SJ Lawry is a Melbourne-based community lawyer, accredited mediator and writer and editor, with expertise in community legal education and training lawyers in plain language communication. She focuses on creative and other non-fiction writing, and is particularly interested in exploring trauma, resilience and relationship. www.7projects.com.au.

Chris Muir lives in Melbourne. He is not an "artist" and feels undeserving of this acknowledgement for his contribution of a "scribble" on page 13.

Susanna Nelson is a journalist, editor and speechwriter across health, the environment, infrastructure, politics and the arts. She likes to travel, knit and go to gigs in her spare time. Unfortunately, she has no spare time; she has kids. www.susannanelson.com

Thuy On is a freelance arts and literary journalist/critic who's written for a range of publications, including *The Age/Sydney Morning Herald*, *The Australian*, *The Saturday Paper*, *Books+Publishing* and ArtsHub. Her first book, the poetry collection *Turbulence*, is out now, by UWAP.

Mark Phillips is a Brunswick writer who has worked as a newspaper journalist, editor and in communications for the union movement. He is the author of *Radio City: the First 30 Years of 3RRR-FM* (The Vulgar Press, 2006).

Arathi Sriprakash currently lives on a road in the UK. She grew up on a cul-de-sac in Darwin, and misses the streets and parades of her share-houses of Melbourne.

Olivia Shenken studies linguistics, archaeology and literature at Monash University. Somehow, warm cups of tea keep spontaneously appearing in her writing. Her work has appeared in *Lot's Wife* and the student anthology *Incisors & Grinders*. She is interested in empathetic speculative fiction and not-too-distant futures, and can be found online at foxtamers.wordpress.com.

Anna Sublet is a freelance writer from Melbourne. Her work has been published in *The Guardian*, *The Age*, *The Sunday Age*, *Domain*, *Sydney Morning Herald*, *Australian Traveller* and *The Footy Almanac*. Her flash memoir stories have been produced for *Memoria* podcast, and her short story Grey Matter was published in *Visible Ink: Trace*. Anna was a 2018 Writers Victoria Glenfern Fellowship recipient and is a non-fiction reader for *Overland*. She likes playing kick-to-kick, surfing and confronting her phobias.

Since obtaining a Masters degrees in medicine, law and arts, **John White** has enjoyed a lifetime of study, travel (to over 100 countries) and patient care. Now retired, he has more time to write and is working on a number of projects. His writing interests include history (especially the Regency period, Asian and ancient history, and the history of art and architecture), creative non-fiction and travel.

Ailsa Wild was a professional acrobat and whip-cracker who ran away from the circus to become a writer. She is now an author, performer and community artist who loves collaboration. Ailsa has written two junior fiction series, 'Squishy Taylor' and 'The Naughtiest Pixie', and is the lead writer of 'Small Friends Books', an illustrated science adventure series. Ailsa's work has appeared in *Meanjin*, *The Monthly*, ABC online and *#METOO: stories from the Australian movement*.

DESIGNER'S NOTES ABOUT THE COVER

The illustration I created for the cover of this book depicts the building material synonymous with Melbourne – bluestone.

If you live in this city long enough it's easy to overlook how much bluestone is around. It is found not only in the famous cobbled laneways of the inner city, but also in the quieter laneways among houses of the surrounding suburbs, not to mention all the kerbs and gutters of the inner suburban streets.

Many of our heritage-listed churches, schools, warehouses, and landmark buildings, such as Pentridge Prison and the Old Melbourne Gaol, as well as more modern buildings such as the National Gallery of Victoria, are all made from this hardy material. As part of my research for the cover design, I did a little digging (no pun intended) into the local history and use of bluestone; here are some of my findings ...

...

What we call "bluestone", otherwise known as basalt or olivine basal, is cooled molten lava. The third largest volcanic basalt plains in the world are located in western Victoria, and they date from 4.5 million years ago. Indigenous knowledge and use of bluestone has been discovered in Melbourne and throughout Victoria; for example, bluestone was used for an eel trap system that has been carbon-dated as being created 6,600 years ago.

Bluestone became a favoured building material during the Victorian gold rush period of the 1850s, leading to all the historic bluestone we see around today. Convict labour was used in bluestone quarries all around the state, as well as those in the inner suburbs of Melbourne. Early Melbourne quarries of the 1830s and 1840s were located in Fitzroy Gardens, Carlton, and Clifton Hill. Further quarries opened in Brunswick, Footscray and Williamstown, followed by Coburg and Preston. As early as the late 1880s, bluestone started to become unfashionable, being seen as sombre and grim. It was superseded by lighter stones such as granite and sandstone as the material of choice for important public buildings.

Bluestone is still quarried and used in a variety of ways today, not just for restoration purposes, but also for commercial and residential developments, modern street pavers and other public infrastructure. Crushed bluestone aggregate, known as "blue metal", remains widely used around Victoria in the likes of concrete making and combined with bitumen for use in road surfacing.

A century-and-a-half from its mid–late nineteenth century heyday, the same bluestone is prized once again, only now for its heritage value. This naturally rough material contributes considerably to the aesthetic of Melbourne; our city would look very different without the blue-grey stone that colours so much of it.

...

Alyssa Coombs

References:

Trig, Stephanie, *From molten lava to cobbled laneways: how bluestone shaped Melbourne's identity*, University of Melbourne, www.findanexpert.unimelb.edu.au/news/2895 (accessed 30 April 2020).

The Australian Research Council of Excellence for the History of Emotions, *Victorian bluestone: an affective cultural history*, www.historyofemotions.org.au/research/research-projects/victorian-bluestone-an-affective-cultural-history/ (accessed 30 April 2020).

Encyclopedia of Melbourne, *Quarries and Brickmaking*, www.emelbourne.net.au/biogs/EM01213b.htm (accessed 30 April 2020).

EDITORS' ACKNOWLEDGEMENTS

Sarah Fraser

When I first came up with the idea of this book, I had two practical aims: I wanted to create an opportunity for writers to get their stories heard, and I wanted make something that people would like to read. But an unexpected outcome of making this book is the micro community that formed around it – it's been a pleasure to work with so many people on a creative endeavour like this. Thank you to all the contributors for your words and enthusiasm. Thanks Sue for being an able co-editor and sounding board, and Alyssa for the fabulous design and cover art. All of your combined efforts have created something we should all be proud of.

And as always, thanks to my family and friends for your support and for generally showing an interest.

...

Susanna Nelson

I would like to thank Sarah and Alyssa for their excellent camaraderie on this journey. Sarah, thank you for keeping me on the straight and narrow, and reminding me of the precious nature of dreams and pet projects in the midst of all the things we do for others and for money. Thanks to all the writers whose lively, heartfelt writing was such a pleasure to edit. I'm grateful for the support of Chris and his bullshit detector, and I dedicate this work to Henry and Gertrude, who no doubt already feel a strong sense of ownership of Melbourne and will be interested to read about the city as it was 'back in our day'.

This book is dedicated to all Melburnians
– past, present and future.

www.ingramcontent.com/pod-product-compliance
Lightning Source LLC
Chambersburg PA
CBHW021701110726
47902CB00007B/2018

9780995446922